CROSSING THE TYNE

Frank Manders and Richard Potts

with an introduction by Professor Norman McCord

and colour photography by Graeme Peacock

TYNE BRIDGE PUBLISHING

A perceptual map (not to scale) of the River Tyne produced by the Tyne Improvement Commission in March 1912.

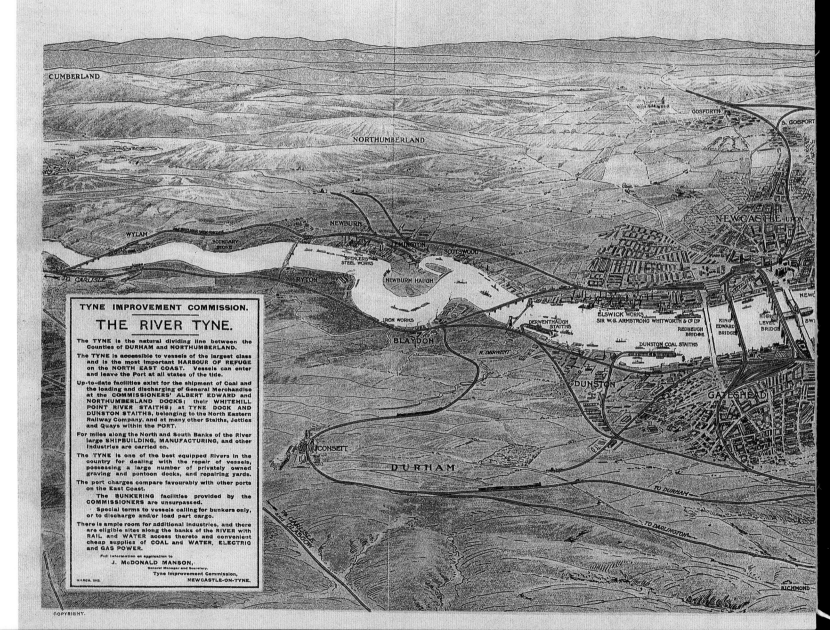

TYNE IMPROVEMENT COMMISSION.

THE RIVER TYNE.

The TYNE is the natural dividing line between the Counties of DURHAM and NORTHUMBERLAND.

The TYNE is accessible to vessels of the largest class and is the most important HARBOUR OF REFUGE on the NORTH EAST COAST. Vessels can enter and leave the Port at all states of the tide.

Up-to-date facilities exist for the shipment of Coal and the loading and discharging of General Merchandise at the COMMISSIONERS' ALBERT EDWARD and NORTHUMBERLAND DOCKS; their WHITEHILL POINT RIVER STAITHS; at TYNE DOCK AND DUNSTON STAITHS, belonging to the North Eastern Railway Company, and at many other Staiths, Jetties and Quays within the PORT.

For miles along the North and South Banks of the River large SHIPBUILDING, MANUFACTURING, and other industries are carried on.

The TYNE is one of the best equipped Rivers in the country for dealing with the repair of vessels, possessing a large number of privately owned graving and pontoon docks, and repairing yards.

The port charges compare favourably with other ports on the East Coast.

The BUNKERING facilities provided by the COMMISSIONERS are unsurpassed.

Special terms to vessels calling for bunkers only, or to discharge and/or load part cargo.

There is ample room for additional industries, and there are eligible sites along the banks of the RIVER with RAIL and WATER access thereto and convenient cheap supplies of COAL and WATER, ELECTRIC and GAS POWER.

Full information on application to
J. McDONALD MANSON,
General Manager and Secretary,
Tyne Improvement Commission,
NEWCASTLE-ON-TYNE.

MARCH, 1912.

COPYRIGHT.

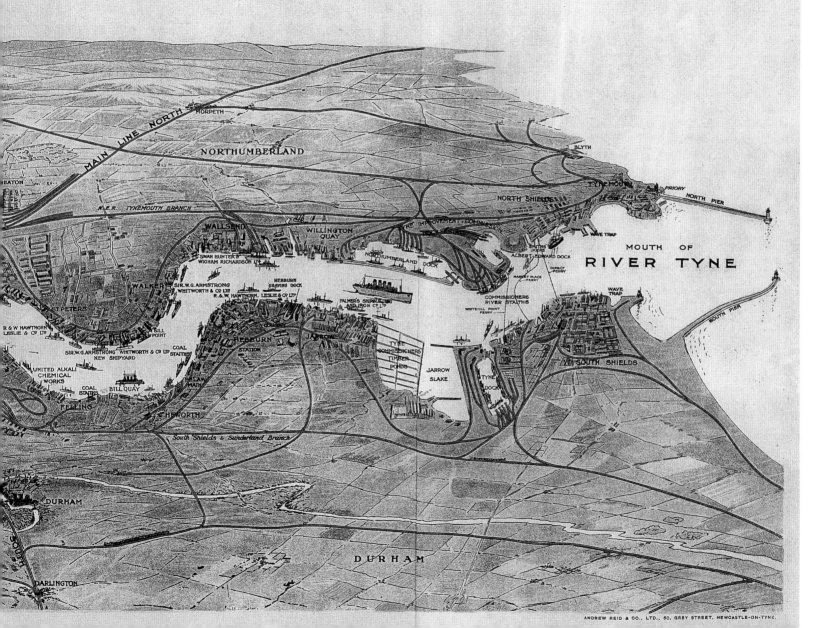

MORPETH

MAIN LINE NORTH

NORTHUMBERLAND

BLYTH

TYNEMOUTH

PRIORY

NORTH PIER

NORTH SHIELDS

N.E.R. TYNEMOUTH BRANCH

WALLSEND

WILLINGTON QUAY

THE IMPROVEMENT COMMISSION

SMITHS DOCKS

WAVE TRAP

SWAN HUNTER & WIGHAM RICHARDSON LTD

NORTHUMBERLAND DOCK

ALBERT EDWARD DOCK

MOUTH OF

RIVER TYNE

MARKET PLACE FERRY

DIRECT FERRY

WALKER

SIR W.G. ARMSTRONG WHITWORTH & CO LTD

HEBBURN GRAVING DOCK

R. & W. HAWTHORN, LESLIE & CO LTD

PALMERS SHIPBUILDING AND IRON CO LTD

COMMISSIONERS RIVER STAITHS

WHITEHILL POINT FERRY

WAVE TRAP

ST PETERS

SOUTH PIER

R & W HAWTHORN LESLIE & CO LTD

BILL POINT

HEBBURN STATION

JARROW

TYNE COMMISSIONERS TIMBER PONDS

SIR W.G. ARMSTRONG WHITWORTH & CO LTD NEW SHIPYARD

COAL STAITHS

JARROW SLAKE

TYNE DOCK

SOUTH SHIELDS

UNITED ALKALI CHEMICAL WORKS

COAL STAITHS

BILL QUAY

PELAW MAIN

FELLING

HEWORTH

South Shields & Sunderland Branch

DURHAM

SOUTH

DURHAM

DARLINGTON

ANDREW REID & CO., LTD., 50, GREY STREET, NEWCASTLE-ON-TYNE.

Acknowledgements

The authors would like to acknowledge the unfailing help and interest of many people in the preparation of this study, in particular the staffs of Newcastle City Library (Local Studies Section) and Tyne and Wear Archives. We wish also to acknowledge the help of the staffs of the Local History sections of the libraries at Gateshead, North Shields and South Shields. Others include Lindsay Allason-Jones, Peter Buchan, Jim Cuthbert, John Dobson, Jimmy Donald, Ron French, Noel Hanson, Nick Hodgson, John Johnson, Dick Keys, Stuart Little, David Potts, Bob Rennison, Allan Seaman, Ken Smith, Ian Wagstaff and the Port of Tyne Authority (especially 'Geordie' Fenwick). We are especially grateful for the encouragement of Anna Flowers, Vanessa Histon and Shawn Fairless of Tyne Bridge Publishing.

Illustrations acknowledgements:
Black and white photographs ©Newcastle Libraries & Information Service except where otherwise indicated.
Colour photographs ©Graeme Peacock except where otherwise indicated.
The OS maps on pages 10, 27, 85, 100 ©Crown copyright. All rights reserved.
Newcastle City Council number LA 076244/01/01
Cover design by Anthony Flowers

Find Tyne Bridge Publishing at
www.newcastle.gov.uk/tynebridgepublishing
Find Graeme Peacock at
www.graeme-peacock.com

Printed by Elanders Hindson, North Tyneside

Tyne Bridge Publishing would like to thank the following for

Newcastle City Council

The Tyne's river crossings lie at the heart of our region, not only as pivotal parts of the road, rail, cycle and footpath networks which link our communities, but also as potent symbols of the North East, held in great affection by its inhabitants. Newcastle City Council takes great pride in managing and maintaining many of these most priceless aspects of our heritage. At a time which has seen the 150th anniversary of the opening of the High Level Bridge, the 50th anniversary of the opening of the Tyne Pedestrian and Cyclist Tunnel and the opening of the new Gateshead Millennium Bridge, it gives me great pleasure to support the publication of a book which celebrates the enormous historical and contemporary importance of the Tyne's river crossings.

John Miller
Head of Planning and Transportation

Gateshead Council

The Tyne has always brought life and prosperity to the region, and especially to the Tyneside conurbation. It is timely then that the publication of this book coincides with a new era for the Tyne. The regeneration of the Gateshead and Newcastle quayside areas heralds a new period of prosperity, the river taking centre stage.

The history and importance of individual river crossings is well documented. As well as their practical importance, the bridges in particular have become the region's landmarks. They are rooted in the area's culture.

With the arrival of the Gateshead Millennium Bridge we have a new landmark, surely the jewel in the Tyne's crown. I wish it and this book long life and great success.

George Gill
Leader of Gateshead Council

their generous support in the production of this book:

Edmund Nuttall Ltd

Edmund Nuttall Ltd. is a long-established major British Civil Engineering construction company, a member of Hollandsche Beton Groep nv [HBG] since 1978. Expertise covers design, construction and maintenance of all types of maritime structures and coastal engineering, roads, bridges, railways, airports, tunnels, public health, dams, pipelines and industrial installations. Proud of its association with the River Tyne, from the construction of the Walker Naval Yard in 1913-23, Nuttall constructed the Tyne Tunnel 1962-3, New Redheugh Bridge 1980-83 and Blaydon Bridge 1988-90. Edmund Nuttall Ltd. looks forward to continued involvement in a forward-looking Tyneside from their local offices in the Newcastle Business Park.

Mott MacDonald

Mott MacDonald is a world class company engaged in development touching many aspects of everyday life – from transport, energy, water and the environment, to building, industry, communications and education. Mott MacDonald are proud to have been established in Newcastle from their early involvement on the Tyne Bridge, through the Tyne Tunnel and Redheugh Bridge, to current involvement with landmark projects such as the Centre for Life and Gateshead Music Centre.

The University of Newcastle upon Tyne

The University's engineering graduates and researchers have a proud tradition of association with the river crossings, including the newest ones. Nowhere else in Britain, and possibly Europe, can one find such a magnificent teaching resource as the impressive and innovative bridges in the centre of Newcastle.

The University of Northumbria at Newcastle

The University of Northumbria is a major contributor to the well-being of the city, both economically and culturally.

Contents

page

Norman McCord

Redheugh Bridge, King Edward VII Bridge, the High Level Bridge, the Swing Bridge, and the Tyne Bridge, c.1950.

Introduction

The invitation to contribute an Introduction to this book was a very welcome one, partly because it gives me an opportunity to record how much all of us who have an interest in the history of North East England owe to the two authors. Their many years of work in local libraries and archives has equipped them with an encyclopaedic knowledge of local sources, and this knowledge has always been generously deployed for the benefit of others working in this field. No doubt much of the evidence gathered here has been sought for this specific purpose, but the diverse sources could only have been brought together by individuals already expert in the varied materials relating to the region's history.

The story of the Tyne's crossings is a matter of great interest to local historians but, as local histories often do, this story also illuminates historical matter of a much more general import. Implicit in the story is the way in which human development on Tyneside continues to be influenced by events which took place in a very remote past, long before the first men and women arrived here. Many millions of years ago, geological developments determined that our main rivers, including the Tyne, should generally follow a west-east direction and this aspect of our inherited natural development lies behind all the complex story discussed in this book and continues to influence our lives powerfully today.

The study of the past is commonly divided into broad categories, bearing such descriptions as political, economic and social history. This detailed study of the Tyne crossings offers a cautionary tale here in its complexity, and in the inter-relations between different elements in the long story. For example, in the past century and a half the area has been transformed in a way which would have astonished earlier generations. The development of modern Tyneside society has owed much to technological and economic change, with the improvement of the Port of Tyne and its crossings being a crucial element. That economic and social transformation of the region could not have been achieved without the involvement of political processes, including the development of towns like Gateshead, Jarrow, Wallsend, North Shields and South Shields to the point where they were politically powerful enough to challenge Newcastle's old monopoly of control of the lower Tyne. Time and again in these pages the reader will find innovators resorting to parliamentary legislation to facilitate bridges, tunnels, and ferries. Local authorities and private interests are frequently found attempting to mobilise political influences in support of their own requirements. This is a story which it is impossible to understand without taking a variety of political, social and economic elements into account.

Those who know something of the range and complexity of the sources drawn upon for this book will appreciate just how much hard work has gone into it, and feel grateful to the authors for this significant contribution to our region's history.

Norman McCord,
Emeritus Professor of Social History,
University of Newcastle upon Tyne.

The High Level Bridge and the Georgian Tyne Bridge from the Gateshead shore, c.1865. The High Level Bridge, opened in 1849, was essential to accommodate the increasing road and rail traffic across the Tyne.

The Tyne at Ryton, just down-river from the tidal stone.

Newburn Bridge.

Blaydon Bridge.

Scotswood Bridge.

Redheugh Bridge.

Redheugh, King Edward VII, Queen Elizabeth II, High Level, Swing, Tyne, and Gateshead Millennium Bridge.

The High Level Bridge by J.W. Carmichael.

High Level, Swing, Tyne, and Gateshead Millennium Bridge.

The Swing Bridge and the Tall Ships, 1996.

The Swing Bridge.

A frosty day, November 2000.

The Tyne Bridge at night.

Millennium celebrations.

Spectators on the Tyne Bridge watch the arrival of the Gateshead Millennium Bridge, 20 November 2000.

sian Hercules II transports the Gateshead Millennium Bridge to its final position.

The new bridge tilts, 28 June 2001.

The Tyne Vehicular Tunnel.

The Tyne Pedestrian Tunnel.

The *Shieldsman* ferry.

Preface

In the autumn of 1983 an exhibition titled 'Crossing the Tyne', was organised by us on behalf of Newcastle Libraries and Tyne and Wear Archives. We were fascinated to discover the amount of human ingenuity, much of it forgotten, which had, over the last 200 years, been devoted to solving the problems posed by the Tyne. Retirement has given us the opportunity to investigate the subject more thoroughly and this book is the result. As non-engineers, we have avoided technical descriptions of bridge building and tunnelling, preferring to concentrate on why the bridges and other structures were built where they were, and on the background to their construction.

We have tried to give equal attention to structures such as the Redheugh and Swing Bridges, previously less well researched than the High Level and Tyne Bridges. Wherever possible, we have gone back to the original sources in archives and libraries in an attempt to give a true record of the building of these structures, uncomplicated by the accretions of local legend.

There have been fords, ferries, bridges, tunnels and other crossings along the entire length of the river, including the North and South Tyne and tributaries. This book however covers only the tidal section, approximately 20 miles administered first by Newcastle Corporation and then from 1850 by the Tyne Improvement Commission (from 30 July 1968 the Port of Tyne Authority), from Hedwin Streams above Ryton down to the sea. There were around 40 different crossing points over this short distance, with at least as many, sometimes ingenious, alternative schemes that remain unfulfilled. Overhead and riverbed cable crossings have been omitted.

The crossings are described geographically, east to west, with the exception of those between Newcastle and Gateshead where we have adopted a chronological approach.

The Tyne was once a difficult river to navigate, particularly for sea-going ships, due to its many small islands, sandbanks, shoals and shallows. Indeed, in the early 19th century it was said that at low tide women could often be seen in midstream pounding clothes or gathering coal. In 1843 an American sailor won a bet by walking across the harbour entrance at Shields. By the 1830s, with the advent of steamboats and industrial growth, Newcastle was conscious of the need to improve the river and access to businesses along its banks. However, it was not until 1850, when responsibility for the river passed to the new Tyne Improvement Commission, representing all the maritime interests and riverside local authorities, that real change occurred.

By 1872 the Admiralty Surveyor reported: 'from being a byeword of neglect and decay, the Tyne has been converted into the most noteworthy example of river improvement within the bounds of the United Kingdom'. Tyne Improvement Commission (TIC) achievements were many, including building the Tyne piers and the Swing Bridge, removing islands and other obstacles, and dredging, widening and straightening the river. Between 1861 and 1914 about 133 million tons of material were removed and dumped at sea. The river up to Newcastle developed into a major maritime thoroughfare, while industry on both banks within the tidal reaches above Newcastle became accessible from the sea for the first time. Imports and exports grew, businesses developed and Tyneside prospered.

In its role as guardian of the Tyne and its shipping, the TIC consistently opposed any scheme which it believed was detrimental to this primary function, even seeking the backing of the Admiralty when necessary.

Richard Potts, Frank Manders, August 2001

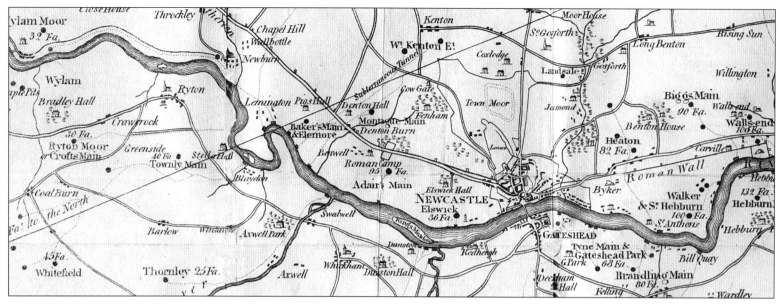

The River Tyne, with no bridges between the Tyne Bridge and Corbridge. From D. Akenhead & Sons' plan of the Rivers Tyne & Wear, 1807.

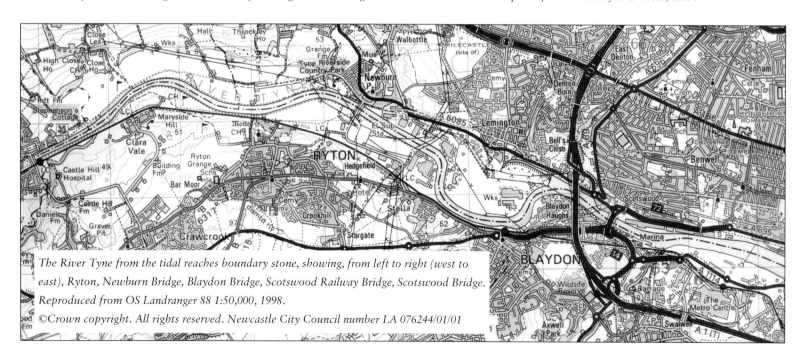

The River Tyne from the tidal reaches boundary stone, showing, from left to right (west to east), Ryton, Newburn Bridge, Blaydon Bridge, Scotswood Railway Bridge, Scotswood Bridge. Reproduced from OS Landranger 88 1:50,000, 1998.

Crossings above Newcastle (from Hedwin Streams)

Ryton Ferry

Ryton ferry was just upstream of an old fish weir and linked River Lane, Ryton, to Ryton Island and the lanes up to Heddon on the Wall and Throckley. The boatman's house was originally on the north bank. In the Great Flood of 1771 (see page 33) the ferryman escaped from an upper window down to a boat sent to rescue him. This old house, known as Island House, was abandoned in the early 20th century, and the new ferry house located on the the south side of the river. An early 20th-century illustration of the ferry shows a small rowing boat. The ferry apparently continued to function until about 1950, and was for many years run by the Scott family. This was the nearest crossing to the Tidal Stone boundary marker at Hedwin Streams (illustrated below).

The Ryton ferryman, Joseph Scott, in 1926 (top), and the Ryton ferry c.1900, with the ferryman's house on the north bank.

The Newburn Fords, Ferry and Bridges

Before dredging and realignment works by the Tyne Improvement Commission, the lowest recognised fordable points across the Tyne were in the Newburn area. There were at least four relatively shallow fords here. Coming downstream, there was Newburn Ford on the approximate line of the present bridge. A short distance below this, and connected to it, was the Riding Ford. Slightly further to the east, and just above the New Burn was the Kelso (Kelshy, or Kelshaw) Ford, a drove-road crossing from Scotland to the south. The Romans are said to have paved the bed of the river here to improve the passage. The fourth and lowest was at Stella Haughs, the Cromwell (or Crummel) Ford. 'Crummel' is said to be Old English for a winding or crooked stream, appropriate to that bend; after the Civil War, it was assumed the name referred to Oliver Cromwell, who crossed there on his way south in 1651 and so it became Cromwell Ford. The Ryton enclosure award of 1800 mentions a Low Ford road, leading from the Spetchels 'near to the ancient ford across the River Tyne called the Low Ford', perhaps the Riding or Kelshaw Ford.

A Scottish army under King David forded the Tyne at Newburn in 1346, on its way to Neville's Cross, where it was defeated. In August 1640, the battle of Newburn occurred here. Twenty thousand Scots were camped at Heddon Law above the village, while 3000 English infantry and 1,500 cavalry were positioned behind hastily-built earthworks along a stretch of meadow on the south bank. The English reckoned that there were eight or ten places there where the Scots might cross. The two main earthworks were directly opposite the two fords where the Scots were most likely to pass at low water. Each was garrisoned by 400 musketeers and four guns. The Scots played a waiting game overnight and the next day, but brought cannon down into Newburn, some of which they placed in the church tower. A Scottish officer, watering his horse,

was shot at and wounded by an English sniper. This set off retaliatory fire, quickly joined by the bigger guns on both sides. The English defences were holed by Scottish artillery, while the English ordnance concentrated in particular on the Scottish guns doing so much damage from Newburn church tower. By the time the Tyne was at low water the Scots had breached the larger English earthwork, inflicting injuries and loss of life. Many of the English retreated and when more were killed the remainder disobeyed their officers' orders and fled. A small troop of Scots forded the river to scout; two regiments of Scottish horse followed. Their Royalist opponents retreated to Ryton and Stella, and then to Newcastle which was taken by the Scots a few days later. The crossing used by the Scots is thought to have been the Cromwell, although this does not satisfy all the known details of the battle.

Almost a century later John Humble, hostman (whose guild controlled the coal trade), petitioned Newcastle Common Council to build a bridge across the Tyne hereabouts. The site was viewed and found acceptable; at its meeting on 25 January 1737 the Council approved his plan subject to safeguards. Unfortunately, the records contain no mention of the proposed location of this unbuilt bridge. John Humble did however possess land on the riverside between Stella and Newburn, and the previous year the Corporation gave him permission to build an extensive quay near the south side of 'the Low Ford'.

In the mid-19th century, the Newburn, Riding and Kelshaw Fords were still in use, and by then a ferry was operating just upstream of Newburn Ford. The ferry continued until a bridge was built nearby. A temporary bridge, apparently of wood, was proposed as early as 1883. The permanent Newburn Bridge was designed by J.W. Sandeman & J.M. Moncrieff of Newcastle (engineers of the second Redheugh Bridge), built for the Newburn Bridge Company by Head Wrightson of Teesside and opened on Whit Monday, 22 May 1893, in time for the Blaydon Races held that day.

It is said that, before dredging in 1873, the river here was so shallow in places that a railway line was laid across the bed of the Tyne to take slag from Spencer's Iron Works to the south side to build up the river bank.

Newburn Bridge from the south-west c.1910, with Spencer's Steel Works in the background.

ⓘ Newburn Bridge

A simple, steel lattice girder structure, with four main spans of 31.5m each, and a 5.5m wide road-deck. The bridge is noteworthy for the depth of its foundations, each of the three piers supported by cylinders of wrought-iron plating filled with concrete, and sunk to a maximum depth of 29.6m below the roadway to rest on solid rock. Newburn Bridge incorporates water and gas mains on each side, as well as telephone cabling. It was until 1947 a toll bridge, with a tollhouse at the north-east end, since demolished.

Blaydon Ford and Ferry

Before the Tyne Improvement Commission improved the river at Blaydon in the 1870s and 1880s, there were two islands, known as Dent's Meadows, reached from the west of the village by a ford. By 1851 a small boat operated as a ferry on a line north east of Blaydon church. Access on both banks was by a flight of steps. A plan 'of the ferry routes at Blaydon' in 1900 shows the lines of 'the old Ferry', a 'disused Ferry' to its west, and 'the present Ferry' to the west of both. The ferry routes were altered because of silting and Tyne Improvement Commission works between Lemington and Blaydon. The ferry seems to have been in existence until the Second World War, linking up on the north bank with a track to Lemington.

Lemington Point Ferry and Bridges

There was a ferry to the east of Lemington Gut, linking Bell's Close and Blaydon Haughs, from late Victorian times. This ferry seems to have been hauled across the river with the assistance of guide ropes. When the horseshoe bend at Lemington was eliminated by the Tyne Improvement Commission in the 1870s it shortened the river by three quarters of a mile and created an island (although Lemington Gut is today a cul-de-sac). An 86.3m long timber footbridge was built in 1916 as a temporary structure inside the Gut to link Lemington Point and Blaydon Haugh; the 15.2m centre span was the same height as the Scotswood Suspension Bridge to enable shipping to reach Throckley coal staith, while the walkways either side of the centre span were just 1.5m above the water. This bridge existed until at least 1953. Both the ferry and the footbridge existed for Armstrong's employees to cross to the munitions works on 'Canary Island', so called because the chemicals used made their skin and hair yellow. In 2001 a new bridge was built across the neck of Lemington Gut to provide access to the new industrial site at Newburn Riverside.

The Lemington Gut footbridge photographed c.1950.

Blaydon Bridge

While considering the abolition of bridge tolls, the Ministry of Transport announced in 1936 that it had been contemplating an additional Tyne crossing and suggested a by-pass west of Newcastle with a new bridge at Scotswood, replacing the suspension bridge. At that early stage, there were proposals for an opening bridge that would carry both rail as well as road traffic. Local authority officers thought the 21.7km by-pass and bridge scheme premature, but considered that the road corridor should be planned in readiness.

The Newcastle Western By-Pass scheme was not included in the Ministry Trunk Road Programme until 1977. Funding for the construction and subsequent maintenance of this stretch of road was deemed a Central Government responsibility. Work on the By-Pass began in the spring of 1987, with the northernmost section being opened three years later. The remaining portion, including the new bridge, was completed a few months afterwards. On Saturday, 1 December 1990, the Queen unveiled a plaque on the bridge, naming it the Blaydon Bridge, and opened the new two-lane dual carriageway road. The entire 11.26km Newcastle Western By-Pass was opened to traffic the following Monday, linking up with the Gateshead Western By-Pass, already constructed. The existing A1 was diverted onto the new road (rejoining the old A1 at North Brunton, while the former route through the Tyne Tunnel became the A19). The road project cost £88 million and was immediately declared a dream for commuters, transforming the lives of motorists long accustomed to traffic-jams. Furthermore, as the local press pointed out, through traffic on the revised A1 now encountered not one roundabout or set of traffic lights over its entire length in the county of Tyne and Wear. Within a few days of opening, the Western By-Pass was carrying 4,000 vehicles an hour at peak times.

Blaydon Bridge

The entire Bypass scheme, including Blaydon Bridge, was designed by Ministry of Transport staff, in conjunction with the consulting engineers, Bullens and Partners, of Durham. The bridge contractors were Edmund Nuttall of Camberley and Newcastle (one of Europe's largest construction firms, through its Dutch parent HBG), and the main contractors for the Tyne Road Tunnel and the present Redheugh Bridge. Nuttalls were awarded the bridge contract, valued at £17 million, in October 1987, began work on 16 November that year, and finished three weeks ahead of schedule, on 30 November 1990. At the time of building, the design of Blaydon Bridge was a first for the United Kingdom, using three balanced cantilevers in parallel. Unexpected problems with the foundation rock beneath the south river pier were overcome by installing mini-piling. When opened, the bridge was, along with another built by Nuttalls in North Wales, the highest of its type in the country.

The Scotswood Railway Bridges

The Newcastle and Carlisle Railway Act of 1829 sanctioned a railway bridge at Scotswood, but it was not built for some years. It opened on 21 May 1839, although passenger services over the bridge did not begin until 21 October that year. Until then, the Newcastle terminus of the line was on the south bank of the Tyne, at Redheugh. Designed by the Railway Company's engineer, John Blackmore, the first Scotswood railway bridge, intended to be a temporary structure, comprised 11 spans each of 18.3m. It had stone abutments, but wooden trestles and a wooden deck, and carried the railway at a height of 10.7m above low water. This skew bridge was on the same site as the present one. By 1859 the bridge was in constant if not frequent use; a traffic census conducted that year logged 80 scheduled passenger, five special passenger, 38 luggage and 39 mineral trains – a total of 162 trains in six days.

This bridge occasioned increasing disquiet. The North Eastern Railway (NER) was seeking to take over the Newcastle & Carlisle line (achieved in July 1862) and commercial interests above Tyne Bridge were concerned about the defective structure at Scotswood. Engineers from London, Newcastle and the Tyne Improvement Commission unanimously condemned it; its timbers were decayed, joints rotted, bolts loose; supplementary props had not improved matters. Trains were forbidden to cross the double-track bridge simultaneously. The structure was dilapidated, totally unsafe, and could not be efficiently repaired. Furthermore, the bridge constituted a serious navigational hazard; boats had been damaged, even sunk, in collisions with the piers, and ice collected round it in winter. The Tyne Improvement Commission wanted a railway bridge that helped, not hindered, the tidal flow, and one that allowed masted vessels to reach industry further upstream. It suggested a swing-bridge replacement.

Following complaints, a Board of Trade inspector, Colonel Yolland, examined the structure on 9 May 1860. The inspector ordered locomotives to be run across throughout the morning to test the bridge's strength and stability. He left before noon. At about 2.30pm hot ash, dropped from an engine hauling a mineral

An engraving by Thomas Hair, drawn by J.W. Carmichael, of the first bridge at Scotswood, built in 1839 of wood. The Suspension Bridge is in the background.

The 1871 Scotswood railway bridge, on the same alignment as its precursor, photographed in 1959. It has been disused since 1982.

train from Newcastle to Carlisle, ignited and within three hours the resulting fire had totally destroyed the timber structure. Inaccurate reporting and subsequent legend then embroidered the incident implying that the bridge was completely burnt down in front of the Government official, but this was not the case. Railway traffic was then diverted over the High Level Bridge and the old line to Blaydon.

In 1861 another wooden bridge was erected. In 1865 the Tyne Improvement Commission declared its willingness to contribute £15,000 towards a satisfactory and permanent replacement. The temporary single-track structure lasted until 1871, when a metal double-track replacement costing £20,000 was opened. In 1888 the NER talked of replacing this further 'temporary' bridge, but nothing was done until it was strengthened in 1943. Although still standing today, from 1982 all traffic was diverted via Dunston.

The elegant lines of John Green's Scotswood road bridge are clearly evident in this view of c.1890. The toll house is at the left.

'A situation more picturesque and striking than the one it occupies could scarcely have been selected for this beautiful bridge, had it only been designed for no other purpose than to adorn the noble Tyne,' said one commentator when the bridge was opened.

The Scotswood Suspension Bridge

Scotswood Suspension Bridge has of course been immortalised in the Geordie anthem:

'Aa went to Blaydon Races, 'twas on the ninth of June
Eighteen hundred and sixty-two on a summer's afternoon…
We flew across the Chine Bridge reet inter Blaydon Toon…'.

The initiative for a permanent crossing in the Scotswood-Lemington area came from the rector of Ryton, Revd. (later Archdeacon) Charles Thorp, who interested several local landowners in a scheme to connect the road on the north bank with the turnpike road from Gateshead to Hexham. Their first meeting took place at the Stella Staith Inn on 23 December 1827. The group's surveyor, William Chapman, prepared a report on potential sites at Newburn, Stella and Scotswood. A bridge at Newburn could not join either the Gateshead-Hexham or the Newcastle roads without creating new highways up steep gradients. A crossing at Stella would be expensive because of the need to by-pass Lemington iron works. A bridge at Scotswood would connect with Newcastle turnpike, and also from there on to Ponteland and Morpeth, while to the south the road could easily be opened up to Gibside, Medomsley, Lanchester and the Derwent Valley. The total cost of the preferred route was estimated at £7,773, including the cost of an enabling Act of Parliament, land for approach roads (including a new Scotswood Road from Forth Banks in Newcastle) and purchasing the ferry (probably the Benwell ferry, but this seems not to have occurred). The bridge alone would cost about £2,700.

A Joint Stock Company was formed in 1828 to build a toll bridge, with separate tolls levied on the approach roads. The Act of Parliament was passed on 13 April 1829, enabling the scheme to go ahead. The legislation, like that for the Newcastle & Carlisle Railway, authorised the shareholders of the two companies to erect a single bridge at Scotswood to carry both road and rail, but the directors of the railway company soon declined to proceed with that idea. To protect its interests, the bridge company had a clause inserted in the Act making it unlawful for any other bridge to be erected within 915m of their crossing, for the passage of horses, cattle and people – except persons travelling in 'railway carriages properly constructed'.

The classic engraving of the Scotswood chain bridge about a year after completion in 1832.

Work soon commenced. The first stones (from Lawson Main Quarry at Byker) of the south abutment were laid on 21 July 1829 under the direction of the Newcastle architect John Green, who is credited with its design. It should however be noted that Captain Samuel Brown issued a warning not to infringe his patent, and it would seem likely that this suspension (or 'chain') bridge was built under licence from him. Flooding on 13 October 1829 resulted in most of the bridge scaffolding being carried away, with a consequent delay in progress. The foundation stone was laid on 9 February 1830. Masonry work was by Welch of Gateshead, and ironwork by Walker & Yates of Birmingham. The first chain was hung across the river on 23 February and the last on 5 March 1831. The two 23.8m high stone suspension towers with entrance arches were well proportioned and were described as 'approaching the Norman style of architecture'. Because of the low clearance, keels had to step their masts to pass underneath. The total cost of the scheme was £15,000.

Scotswood Suspension Bridge was opened with much jubilation on Tuesday, 16 April 1831. 'The day being particularly fine, and the people's minds greatly excited towards the novel experience of a Bridge of the above construction, the attendance was exceedingly numerous'. On the firing of a signal gun from the Castle Keep, a grand procession of about 90 carriages and gigs, headed by the Mayor of Newcastle and other civic dignitaries, the Committee of Management and shareholders, followed by many gentlemen riding on horseback, set off from the Assembly Rooms in Newcastle, with a band playing and banners waving, along the new Scotswood Road to the just-completed bridge. When they reached the bridge, at 1.30pm, a nine-gun salute was fired. The cavalcade proceeded on to the bridge gingerly, at intervals of 18.3m. Weight concerns were paramount, as a similar bridge had collapsed at Middlesbrough a few months before. Halfway across, the procession halted whilst

the Revd. Charles Thorp dedicated the structure. The opening party continued to Blaydon, Swalwell, and then returned over the bridge to a banquet at the Assembly Rooms, where a commemorative silver tankard was presented to John Green in recognition of his architectural work and supervision.

As soon as the Suspension Bridge was open to the public: 'it was immediately crowded to excess, and was scarcely perceived to yield under the pressure, which plainly shows that it is almost capable of bearing any weight, and which precludes any further necessity of precaution … The neatness and the strength combined, of the above Bridge, is not surpassed by any other of the same construction in the kingdom'. One contemporary estimated that there were perhaps 3,000 people standing on the roadway between the points of suspension, with 2,000 more on the two end-sections! During the day ships on the river were decorated with bunting, and churches joined in the celebrations with peals of bells.

The Mayor and Corporation of Newcastle had an early financial interest in the bridge and roads, purchasing the first 20 shares in the Scotswood Bridge Company on 13 August 1831. By 1870 Newcastle Tramways wished to extend westwards through Scotswood to Newburn (with a single track over the bridge to Blaydon), but were unable to do so whilst Scotswood Road remained in private hands. It was for this reason, the investment potential (and, initially, because it might help to bring Benwell within the city boundaries), that Newcastle eventually bought the entire undertaking by Act of Parliament for £36,500, after some years of negotiation. Control passed into Newcastle's hands on 30 December 1905, although the tram service to Blaydon never came about. Northumberland and Durham County, and Gateshead Borough, Councils paid a proportion of the purchase price for approach roads. The bridge was given county status in 1907 and at 4pm on 18 March that year tolls ceased on both the bridge and

An early lorry crosses the Scotswood road bridge in 1910.

roads formerly belonging to the Scotswood Bridge Company.

As early as 1865, the Tyne Improvement Commission wished to deepen the Tyne above Newcastle. They proposed spending £5,000 for a floating steam bridge to replace the Suspension Bridge, which prevented sea-going vessels getting to the upper tidal reaches. In 1883 Newcastle's engineer, W.G. Laws, warned the Bridge Company that serious rusting had occurred in the chain anchorages below high water and he recommended that these be concreted up to this level, to halt corrosion for between 20 and 30 years, by which time the bridge would probably be replaced by a swing or floating structure. Although Laws calculated that the stress upon the chains was well within the breaking strain of 24 tons per square inch, he felt the number of people on the bridge at any one time should be limited to 3,000! He also recommended supplementary anchors, and a stronger roadway when next renewed – not least because contemporary bridges carried heavier loads than 50 years before. In his view, the real solution lay in bridge reconstruction rather than superficial repair.

In the 1890s an engineer's report resulted in further structural overhaul, with new chains and anchors being bedded in concrete. By 1906 repairs were again needed, including steel replacements for the original wrought-iron suspension rods. From this time on, weight restrictions (limited to 6 tons) were enforced with watchmen preventing unauthorised loads crossing the bridge. Repairs were also required when vessels collided with the bridge, as happened on Christmas Eve, 1898. According to the official report, the loaded collier *Vernon* left Derwenthaugh Staiths about 10.30pm, and was carried by the flood tide underneath the Scotswood Suspension Bridge, losing her masts and funnel, and damaging the bridge. In fact, the captain and pilot had gone ashore and drunk too much; in the meantime the first mate (on bad terms with his skipper, but deciding on a Christmas 'good turn'), turned the vessel round,

 A Highly Successful Bridge

The Management Committee had no prospect of disposing of its mortgage until 1855, when it was announced that tolls were increasing, a contingency fund was envisaged - and a dividend of four per cent was declared. The following year the mortgage was paid off; bridge toll receipts had totalled £1,027 and bridge repairs £134; road tolls yielded £783 and road maintenance cost £670. By 1861 bridge toll receipts had increased to £1,130, road tolls to £815, while the expense of maintaining both bridge and roads was just £634; not surprisingly, with this turnaround in the company's fortunes, the dividend was allowed to rise to six per cent. The average annual dividend over the 40 years before 1903 was 7.25 per cent.

A census of traffic using the bridge, taken from Monday to Saturday, 1-6 August 1859 (at the same time as one for Scotswood Railway Bridge), recorded 2,009 pedestrians, 120 horses and riders, 25 coaches, 239 carriages, 803 carts, 56 wagons, 39 head of cattle and 59 sheep passing over the bridge. The tolls at that time varied between a penny and two shillings, according to the type of user. Stagecoaches and other public carriages paid every time they used the bridge, although same-day return trips were otherwise free of charge.

ready to return to sea; when the captain and pilot returned they again turned the ship round, set sail and fetched up underneath Scotswood Bridge!

By 1928 it was increasingly unsuitable for modern traffic, but it was still possible to comment that: 'It excels all the other bridges

The utilitarian replacement for the Scotswood road bridge alongside its doomed predecessor in June 1966.

[on the Tyne] in the beauty of its design and the slender grace of its span'.

In 1931 extensive repairs and strengthening, to the design of Mott, Hay, and Anderson, were undertaken by Dorman, Long & Company, to allow maximum loads of ten tons, at a cost of about £30,000. Further repairs were necessary as late as 1961, by which time the crossing speed was limited to 10mph.

The moment the new Scotswood Road Bridge was opened, the Suspension Bridge was closed for demolition, despite vigorous attempts to preserve it as one of the earliest suspension bridges in the world. But perhaps the last laugh was with a 10-year old boy, David Dalus. The privilege of being the very last people to cross the old Scotswood Suspension Bridge had been reserved for the civic dignitaries attending the opening of the new road bridge, on 20 March 1967. They were however denied this when David sneaked across on his bicycle behind the official party!

Scotswood Road Bridge (1967)

Replacing Scotswood Suspension Bridge was considered desirable well before 1900, and essential by 1921. However, economic pressure led to a much cheaper programme of limited widening and reconstruction instead. In April 1941 Mott, Hay, and Anderson produced a report for a Joint Committee of Durham and Northumberland County and Newcastle City Councils for a new twin-roadway, high-level bridge, with a 114.4m main span, 25.6m above high water, west of the Suspension Bridge. Discussions continued for another 20 years, including considerations of site and whether the replacement structure should be at high or low level. As late as July 1959 Mott, Hay, and Anderson surveyed the old bridge and gave it a restricted use of just three years. Then in 1960 the Department of Transport finally authorised the building of a new bridge 91.5m west of the Suspension Bridge, with provision for

Scotswood Bridge facts

The Scotswood Bridge Act, authorising Durham County Council and Newcastle Corporation to commission this structure, received the Royal Assent in 1962, and work began on 18 September 1964. It was completed ahead of schedule, at a final cost (including earthworks and viaducts, the new bridge, a reconstructed railway bridge, and demolition of the old suspension bridge) of more than £2.5 million, of which 75 per cent was Government grant. The bridge was opened, with four lanes, on 20 March 1967 by Alderman Peter Renwick, chairman of the Scotswood Bridge Joint Committee. Traffic was diverted off the old suspension bridge and on to the new crossing the same day.

Scotswood Bridge was designed by Mott, Hay, and Anderson and erected by a consortium of Mitchell Construction Kinnear Moodie Group Ltd., with Dorman Long supplying and erecting the steelwork. Overhead electricity cables had to be diverted before construction began, and the bridge carries telephone cables and gas, water and sewer mains.

six carriageways, at an estimated cost of just under £1.5 million.

The twin-arch ribs were originally tied with wire cables that quickly corroded; tie bars were put in their place. One authority described it as a 'very lively bridge, which has regularly been repaired and modified since it opened'. The pedestrian subways frequently flooded in the first years. More seriously, after accidents to other box-girder bridges in Wales, Australia and Germany, resulting in more than 50 fatalities, 51 British box-girder bridges were inspected and 32 found faulty. The centre span at Scotswood is not typical box-girder, but the approaches were built to designs later found unsatisfactory. Because of this crisis traffic was restricted to single file each way between June 1971 and January 1974; fresh strengthening work was done by Cleveland Bridge and Engineering, and cost £436,200. Further repairs were carried out in 1979-1980, and again in 1983. As soon as Blaydon Bridge was opened at the end of 1990, Trunk Road status was removed from Scotswood Bridge, and the following year it was closed to all vehicles (but not pedestrians) for several months while further essential repairs were carried out.

The irritations of constant delays for intermittent major and minor remedial work generated nostalgia for the old suspension bridge despite its shortcomings, particularly weight and speed restrictions. One writer commented: 'beautiful Scotswood Suspension Bridge has been destroyed and in its place now stands an uncompromisingly ugly modern construction. The present bridge developed faults immediately after being built and for a long time has only carried single-line traffic. At the time of writing the only progress is in the cost of repair which rises every few months … [it is] probably cheaper to knock it down … and rebuild. If so, let's hope some element of beauty surreptitiously creeps in at the second attempt'.

The Benwell Ferry

A deed for the manor of Benwell, dated 1770, mentions the Boat Green there and 'the Boat upon the River Tyne' in the tenancy of William Joplen, who paid a yearly rent of £19. In 1805 William Ord of Fenham leased land at Scotswood to various individuals for a paper works, excepting the boathouse and access to and from the ferry landing called 'the Benwell Ferry Boat'. A history of Ryton suggests that as there was no bridge between Corbridge and Newcastle from 1538 when Bywell Bridge was destroyed, to 1831 when Scotswood Suspension Bridge was built, Rytonians wishing to get to Newcastle by road had to use either 'the Scotswood Ferry' or travel along the south bank of the river to the Tyne Bridge. The Benwell Ferry ran from south of the Boathouse (later a public house), west of Paradise, across by sculler boat to Derwenthaugh, and seems to have continued until about the Second World War.

'O where is the boatman . . . My bonny honey!
O where is the boatman . . . Bring him to me -
To ferry me over the Tyne to my honey,
And I will remember the boatman and thee.'

This painting of the 1860s shows the Tyne looking west from the grounds of Redheugh Hall, with the Redheugh branch of the Newcastle and Carlisle Railway on the left. King's Meadows is in the centre, with Clarence Island at its right. A steam tug pulls a string of barges up-river. Part of Elswick Works appears on the right.

Crossings between Newcastle and Gateshead

The Elswick Ferries

There used to be two sizeable islands in the Tyne in front of Armstrong's Elswick works: King's Meadows (about 12 ha) and the Clarence (or Annie) Island (about 0.6 ha). The larger, King's Meadows, was about 1.6 km in length and 137.2m wide, with its eastern extremity off the mouth of the river Team. It had a farm, public house (the Countess of Coventry) and adjoining tea-garden, and was well-known for the horse, running, rowing and swimming races held there. Sir Andrew Noble is said to have carried out gunnery experiments, leading to ordnance patents, there. Before about 1883, it was possible to 'plodge' on foot from Elswick to King's Meadows at low tide. Two illustrations of 1864 show a rowing boat used to convey people and goods from Elswick to King's Meadows.

In 1929 a former publican's daughter or employee recalled her younger days on the island: 'my sister and I rowed hundreds of men to the shore and back again. Many a time I've managed the sculling boat alone with seven or eight drunken men as passengers. All the beer and even water had to be rowed across'. The ferry charge was said to be a halfpenny across to King's Meadows and sixpence back!

Until the Tyne Improvement Commission removed the islands in 1885-1886, there was no ferry linking Elswick and Dunston. A boat between the two was formally proposed in 1894, and by 1899 this was in operation, carrying about 750 people daily in a sculler boat from near the middle of Elswick Works to a point east of the former Dunston Engine Works. In 1896 Newcastle Corporation wanted to establish a steam ferry but the Tyne Improvement Commission opposed this. Newcastle then encouraged the Tyne Improvement Commission to start a horse and cart ferry on this route, but this was never achieved. The sculler boat ferry continued until the 1940s, the last reference found being about 1945. For a relatively short time, perhaps between 1896 and 1940, there was also a Low Elswick ferry service from the east end of Elswick Works/Water Street across to a point east of the CWS Flour Mills at Dunston.

The Tyne from Elswick to beyond St Anthony's showing Redheugh, King Edward VII, Queen Elizabeth II, High Level, Swing and Tyne Bridges. ©*Crown copyright. All rights reserved. Newcastle City Council number LA 076244/01/01*

Bridges between Newcastle and Gateshead, from the earliest times

The Roman Bridge (Pons Aelius)

The first known bridge crossed the Tyne where the tidal river could easily be spanned. This Roman bridge was 'Pons Aelius', taking its title from the emperor Hadrian (family name 'Aelius'). It was built around 122 AD, roughly on the line of the present Swing Bridge. The fort at Newcastle is of a later date than the bridge, and was named after the bridge, but there is evidence of a Roman fort at Bottle Bank, Gateshead. The bridge was probably a wooden deck platform, about 5.5m wide, resting on stone piers, like those found at Corbridge and Chesters on the North Tyne, and elsewhere in Britain and Europe.

The piers were built on a foundation of iron-shod oak piles, perhaps re-inforced with a wooden coffer-dam consisting of two or more retaining walls of posts or planks, packed with watertight clay. Traces of the piers and their supports were found in the river during the building of later structures, notably the Swing Bridge.

An artist's impression of how the Roman Bridge, and the fort of Pons Aelius might have looked.

'Pons Aelius' was perhaps 224.2m in length, for at that time there were no riverside buildings or quays narrowing the Tyne. Two matching altars, dedicated to Oceanus and Neptune (now in Newcastle University's Museum of Antiquities), were also found on the bed of the river during preparatory work for the Swing Bridge. These altars were perhaps set up by the Sixth Legion to protect the bridge. For the next three centuries, until about 410 AD, when they withdrew to protect the heart of their empire, Roman troops held the Wall and bridge against the Northern tribes.

The medieval Tyne Bridge

Some texts suggest that Picts or Scots destroyed 'Pons Aelius', and that after the Roman bridge no permanent structure existed on this site until after the Norman Conquest, but there is little evidence for this. The Roman bridge was a sturdy structure judging by its piling. It seems likely that the Roman bridge continued in use, except when the depredations of invaders, or the ravages of time and weathering, compelled its closure while stone piers were rebuilt or timber decking was renewed. King Athelstan is believed to have crossed the bridge at Newcastle on his way to and from the battle of Brunanburgh in 937, and William the Conqueror passed over it with his army in 1072 to battle with the Scottish king, Malcolm. On his return south William was unable to cross the river by bridge or ford, as the Tyne was then in full flood. The bridge may have been rebuilt when William's son Robert erected the 'New Castle' in 1080, but the evidence is flimsy. The earliest documentary references to a bridge are in the Pipe Rolls (Court of Chancery) for 1179 and 1184.

Tradition has it that the medieval Tyne Bridge was built soon after a disastrous fire largely destroyed a predecessor in 1248. However, the medieval, stone bridge was perhaps erected by the late 12th century. Evidence for this lies in the dedication of the chapel on the bridge to St Thomas à Becket, murdered in Canterbury cathedral in 1170. It has even been suggested that the chapel on the bridge could have been built in expiation by Hugh de Morville, one of the knights who killed Becket.

After the 1248 fire, the Tyne Bridge was rebuilt on the same site, perhaps using some materials from the earlier structure. Newcastle and the Bishop of Durham co-operated in the work, the Bishop and other clergy selling indulgences (remissions of time spent in purgatory after death) in exchange for money, labour and materials. In 1339, a major flood resulted in the drowning of over 100 people (perhaps as many as 167) in Newcastle, the destruction of 140 houses, and severe damage to the bridge. Repairs were also required in 1370.

The bridge originally spanned the river with 12 'bold' or pointed (Gothic) arches, several of which were 'rounded' during subsequent repairs. Three of the arches were filled in and used as storage cellars when quays were built on both banks. The bridge piers were massive, some of them 7m thick; at least a third of the river was obstructed by solid masonry, greatly hindering the flow of water, particularly in abnormal conditions. This perhaps contributed to the bridge's eventual collapse.

The old Tyne Bridge presented an imposing and picturesque appearance, with its towers, shops, houses, and at least one chapel, built somewhat haphazardly upon it, overhanging the river and narrowing the roadway. Some commentators have exaggerated the number of buildings. They were built only on the piers and not above the arches of the Newcastle section, but there were continuous rows on both sides at the Gateshead end. The bridge had a long, prosperous existence as a trading and residential area as well as a means of crossing the river.

One tower was at the southern end with the Bishop's arms, and at one time a portcullis, a drawbridge, and a gate – the 'gate's head', or bridgehead to the south. The 'middle' tower (also with a portcullis, royal arms until 1636, and Newcastle's arms), was on the pier between the third and fourth arches from Newcastle. It was used as a store for the town armour and a prison for lesser offenders ('lewd and disorderly persons till examined by the Mayor and brought to punishment, unless the crime be of gross nature when removed to Newgate'). At the northern end stood the 'Magazine Tower' or gunpowder store, probably built in 1636, and carrying the royal arms. The three towers were used on occasion to resist armed invaders as well as turning round unwelcome travellers including those with plague or disease. The chapel, dedicated to St Thomas à Becket, was at the Newcastle end of the bridge, on the east side. 'Our Lady's Chapel', is said to have existed at one time, also on the east side, and there may once also have been a hermitage.

Initially, the whole bridge was in the custody and care of a Master or Keeper appointed by Newcastle. In 1342, it was declared that 'as the Bridge of Tyne … is in danger of breaking, falling down and being lost, because the rents due to the aforesaid Bridge are withdrawn or detained, it is ordered that the Master of the Bridge … with the aid of [the Newcastle Guilds etc.] … levy the rents and arrears due to the said Bridge without sparing any person [and] … expend them in [its] working, direction and repair'. Gifts of land were made to 'God and the Bridge', 'the Bridge of Tyne' and 'the Proctor of the Bridge of Tyne', who was often also the keeper of St Thomas' Chapel. In 1403 Henry IV granted money (three years after giving Newcastle county status) for the support, alteration and repair of the town's walls and bridge.

Responsibility for the maintenance of the medieval bridge slowly evolved so that it was shared between the town of Newcastle and the Prince-Bishop of Durham. There was frequent friction, despite two elongated, blue marble stones 'St Cuthbert's stones', placed on the third pier from Gateshead, to mark the boundary between the two jurisdictions. Newcastle was keen to control the whole bridge, as by royal grant it had control (or 'conservatorship') of the entire river, including both banks, from Hedwin Streams (just above Ryton) down to Spar or Sparrow Hawk (Tyne Bar and the sea). Even though it would cost more, Newcastle's view was that it made no sense to look after all its stretch of the Tyne, and yet only have responsibility for part of the bridge.

The Bishop also had ambitions, and in 1335 claimed the town of Gateshead was entitled to hold a market and fair as far as the middle of the bridge each year. Around 1383 Newcastle removed the blue stones and built a tower on the Bishop's section, claiming the entire bridge lay within its territory. Frequent squabbling culminated in a lengthy court case at York. In 1413 the Bishop claimed he had always owned the southern half of the bridge and the soil under the Tyne. In 1416 the court delivered its verdict: the Bishop was entitled only to the southern third of the bridge and no part of the river bed; but Newcastle had trespassed, and was made to pay

An engraving by John Hilbert of the Tyne Bridge in 1727, looking up-river. The solid block of buildings is on the Bishop of Durham's part of the structure. The arches appear much higher than they actually were.

heavy damages to the Bishop, restore the blue stones to their correct position, and relinquish the tower now enhancing the Bishop's end of the bridge. The Bishop of Durham from this time on had three and a half piers and four arches, while Newcastle town had five and a half piers and six arches.

In 1553, during a time of religious upheaval, Newcastle petitioned the king for authority to take over the south end of the bridge because of its ruinous condition, so Newcastle briefly acquired the section of the bridge it had long sought – as well as responsibility for the town of Gateshead. Just months later, the Protestant Edward VI died and was succeeded by his Catholic sister, Mary, who quickly reversed the decision.

Despite contributions from the Guild companies, the Tyne Bridge was a constant drain on both the Corporation's and the Bishop's resources. In 1564, for example, large quantities of stone, iron, lead and wood were used by masons, smiths and carpenters for work about the bridge, from basic piling to 'mending a holl of the tynne bridge'. The repairs may have been dangerous for the workmen, for there are references to a 'boott for watchying the masons on the bridge'. In 1582 the Bishop disputed his liability for bridge maintenance, attempting to make the county of Durham responsible instead; a commission found against him. In September 1592 the 'pillars' of the bridge were strengthened with additional stonework and both iron and timber supports. This was evidently an important restoration for boats were hired to convey 'My Lord President, Mr Mayor and his brethren' to inspect the bridge repairs, which took eight weeks to complete.

In 1646 timber was used to repair an arch. By July of the following year, stone and woodwork were again inspected, costs calculated and a report made; three days later the masons and carpenters were ordered to start work on the bridge 'with all expedition'. The emergency repairs were evidently insufficient, for two years

later the Common Council, Newcastle's governing body, petitioned Parliament 'that whereas the King allowed the Town a proportion of trees out of Chopwell woods for the repairing of the bridge, and Parliament had done likewise: but since the bridge had fallen into a ruinous state they petitioned for a grant of the forty trees marked for the king's use', or as many as possible. In January 1656 the Council ordered 'the decayed portions of Tyne Bridge be viewed by Mr Mayor and order given for repair'. In 1639, with Civil War threatening, a recommendation was made to reinstate the drawbridge towards the south end of the Tyne Bridge, to be opened in daytime and closed at night.

James VI of Scotland had passed over the Tyne Bridge ('its manner and beautie … being one of the best in the north parts') on his way south from Edinburgh to London in 1603 to claim the English crown, and his statue and Charles I's arms had been erected on the Magazine Tower. In 1651, with Oliver Cromwell and Parliament firmly in control of the country, 'the late king's arms and portraits of King James were by order of parliament taken down from the new building upon the bridge and the commonwealth arms … set up in the same place instead'. The Common Council approved the words of a Latin inscription (also 'englished') condemning royal privilege and defining 'true liberty'. After the Restoration, a statue of Charles II was placed on the tower, where it remained until 1770, when both tower and monument were removed.

About 1725, Daniel Defoe recorded: 'Newcastle … is seated upon the… Tyne … here a noble, large and deep river, and ships of any reasonable burthen come safely up to the very town … the parts are joined by a very strong and stately stone bridge of seven [*sic*] very great arches, rather larger than the arches of London Bridge, and the bridge is built into a street of houses also, as London Bridge is'. Twenty years earlier, another famous traveller,

The Tyne Bridge after the floods of November 1771.

Celia Fiennes, described the bridge in similar vein, commenting especially on the proliferation of buildings at the Gateshead end. Since 1698, the bridge had carried water pipes supplying Newcastle from Gateshead.

In 1769, the Bishop of Durham employed John Smeaton, builder of the Eddystone lighthouse, to assess the condition of the southern portion. Smeaton's report was unflattering, describing the bridge as 'originally ill built … impossible to render it sound unless the whole was new built … yet by occasional repairs, it may last'. Immediate superficial repairs would cost £150-£200, and these were done on 15-19 July 1770, when ferryboats provided a substitute service. The following year Smeaton advised Newcastle on its sec-

tion, again describing the bridge as 'ill built', 'decayed', and counselling a new bridge. Amongst many defects, he discovered masonry damage caused by coal-carrying keels colliding with the bridge, shearing off ribs on arches and leaving the stonework above dangerously unsupported. Smeaton reckoned this could easily fall and risk the lives of those travelling under the bridge in boats. However, nothing was put in hand before a more serious disaster struck.

The medieval bridge was destroyed later that year by a flood exceeding anything previously known although there had been severe flooding in 1703, 1752 and 1763. Heavy rain fell upstream from the evening of Friday 15 to the morning of Sunday 17 November 1771. By midnight on Saturday, the water had risen so high, about 2.7m above the usual spring-tide level, that it filled all the bridge arches, and covered an area from the west of the Close, the Sandhill, and Newcastle Quayside down almost to the Ouseburn. That evening, flooding was so rapid that those who slept in low-lying property escaped only with difficulty, as cellars and the lower parts of private dwellings, shops and warehouses were inundated. Ships and keels were driven from their moorings, and at least four were beached on the quay.

'But what completed the public calamity was the demolition of Tyne Bridge, which, after having stood the brunt of ages, yielded to the force of the flood.' Early on Sunday morning the middle arch fell; by afternoon two arches near the Gateshead side were so shattered that they, and most houses and shops upon them, fell into the river a few days later. The shops and houses remaining on these sections and one more arch were irreparably damaged. Many traders lost their entire stocks, while those of others were removed only with considerable risk. Collapsed walls and roofs, as well as furniture and goods, joined timber and debris already rushing downstream in a raging torrent. One wooden dwelling floated as far as Jarrow Slake. Had the catastrophe occurred during working hours, hundreds of people might have been killed, but just six died. In one case, a shopkeeper, his wife and maidservant escaped to the Gateshead side where the girl, realising she had left something behind, persuaded her employer to return with her. An arch collapsed under them and they were not seen again. The fifth, seventh, eighth and ninth arches all collapsed, with the worst damage at the Gateshead end, whose short section contained the majority of the bridge's buildings – by 7 December all 21 houses there had gone. The Newcastle section had just 19 buildings upon it, many now damaged beyond repair.

Every bridge on the Tyne, the North Tyne and the South Tyne (excepting only Corbridge, built 1674), was destroyed that week-end, with the loss of animal and some human lives as well as much damage to property, notably at Bywell and Ovingham. Several vessels sank or went aground at Shields, but on the whole the lower reaches escaped relatively lightly. The same catalogue of death and destruction, boats swamped, bridges and river banks broken, buildings demolished and even collieries flooded, occurred on the Wear (notably Barnard Castle, Durham and Sunderland), Tees (Yarm and Stockton) and Skerne (Darlington), and as far away as Cumbria (Carlisle, Appleby and Kendal). Throughout the area, the sheer volume of water cascading downstream, together with uprooted trees and bulky debris, had a devastating effect.

Parts of the land arches of the medieval Tyne Bridge still exist, at least in part: one supposedly under Bridge Street, Gateshead, and one reached from the cellar of the Casa restaurant in Watergate Buildings at the Newcastle end of the Swing Bridge. The section at the Newcastle end is a scheduled ancient monument and includes part of the 18th-century bridge.

According to some commentators the 1771 flood is said to have given Newcastle a shot in the arm, just when it needed it most: 'Newcastle might not have become the handsome city of today but for the fall of the old Tyne Bridge'.

The Georgian Tyne Bridge

The fall of the medieval bridge was a major disaster not quickly or easily remedied. While the town and the surrounding area recovered from the shock, stopgap measures were needed. The first arrangements were doubtless informal, with boat owners running ferry services; but within ten days an official free ferry was operating between the Sandhill and Gateshead, to ensure the mails were carried. Newcastle Common Council then appointed a committee to supervise, manage and administer its ferries and the building of a temporary bridge. The Bridge Committee first met on 13

December 1771, when it approved ferry dues, engaged collectors, and ordered lamps to be lit at night at the ferry landings at Newcastle and Gateshead. After complaints, rules for the ferrymen were introduced in January 1772. Soon afterwards, Newcastle bought new ferryboats, large enough to carry vehicles across the river, including the London-Edinburgh stagecoaches. The new ferries sometimes (according to a seasoned traveller, the Revd. James Murray) took an hour to cross, perhaps due to the debris.

Engineers were consulted, two of whom considered the old bridge a total loss, being too narrow and the approaches too awkward, and recommended a temporary bridge lasting seven years to connect the old remnants. New bridges at a raised level were also suggested. There were many arguments with the Bishop of Durham hinging on the question of rents, or lack of them, for possible houses on a new bridge. In the end cost dictated that a new bridge would be built in the same location as the old one.

The local newspaper later reported that the Corporation and the Bishop had agreed to build a bridge in the same position as the old, 7.3m wide, with arches some 91.4 cms higher than its predecessor.

On 17 March 1772, the Newcastle Committee accepted that a temporary bridge could not rest upon what remained of the old foundations and £2,400 was set aside for building an interim, temporary, bridge and purchasing land and houses in Gateshead for an approach road.

The river began to be cleared of debris and timber was ordered for the temporary bridge – the blue 'bounder' stones

A list of tolls and fares payable on the ferry established by the town and county of Newcastle soon after the 1771 flood.

Town and County of Newcastle upon Tyne.

AT a COMMON COUNCIL, held the 31st Day of December, 1771, It is order'd, that the RATES or FARES, hereafter mentioned, be demanded and taken for crossing the River *Tyne* in the Corporation Ferries, and that the same do commence on Monday the 6th of January next, and continue till the Common Council shall order the contrary : *viz.*

	s.	d.
For every Coach, Chariot, Berlin, Calash, or Landau	1	6
For every Four-wheel Chaise	1	0
For every Two-wheel Chaise	0	6
For every Broad-wheel Waggon, empty	1	6
For every Narrow-wheel Waggon, empty	1	0
For every Wain, with two Horses and Driver	0	2
For the same, if loaded with Coals, Corn, Bread, or Flour	0	2
For the same, if loaded with or carrying any other Goods	0	4
For every Cart, with one Horse and Driver	0	1
For the same, if loaded with Coals, Corn, Bread, or Flour	0	1
For the same, if loaded with or carrying any other Goods	0	2
For every Horse, Mule, or Ass, and Driver	0	1
For the same, if carrying Coals, Corn, Bread, or Flour	0	1
For the same, if carrying any other Goods	0	1½
For Black Cattle per Head	0	1
For every Calf	0	0½
For Swine per Head	0	1
For Sheep per Head	0	0½
For every Passenger, except Children under Eight Years of Age	0	0½
For every Horse-pack	0	1
For every Sack of Flour not in Carts	0	0½
For every Firkin of Butter	0	0¼
For every Crate of Earthen Ware	0	1
For every Hogshead of Tallow, Sugar, Treacle, or other Goods	0	4
For every Pipe or Butt of Beer, or other Liquor	0	4
For every Hogshead of ditto	0	2
For every Half Hogshead or Barrel of ditto	0	1½
For every Half Barrel of ditto	0	1
For every Quarter Barrel of ditto	0	0½
For every Cwt. of Iron, Steel, or Lead	0	0½
For every Parcel of Iron Steel, or Lead, under a Cwt.	0	0¼
For every Cwt. of all other Goods, Wares, or Merchandize, not rated above	0	1
For every Parcel of ditto, under a Cwt.	0	0½

N. B. Waggons are not to pass loaded.

By Order,

GIBSON.

and their position were carefully preserved.

On 14 April, the Committee approved the wording of the Parliamentary Bill. The preamble to the Act passed in 1772 shows the importance of the Tyne crossing: 'Whereas a great part of the Stone Bridge over the River Tyne at Newcastle was destroyed by the violence of a most extraordinary Flood on the 17th Day of November 1771 and thereby the principal Passage from the Northern to the Southern Parts of the Kingdom is in a great Measure obstructed'. The Act stated the temporary bridge was to be as near its predecessor as possible, to make use of surviving arches and piers where practicable; the piers of the interim bridge were to be in line with those of the old, to allow the free flow of water and not weaken either structure; no buildings were to be erected on the temporary bridge, apart from tollhouses; tolls were to continue until Newcastle had recouped its outlay; no loaded wagon drawn by four or more horses was permitted to cross the temporary bridge, because of the narrow width; the term of the Act was to expire on 24 June 1779; if the old bridge was reinstated (or replacement built) sooner, then the temporary bridge was to be removed immediately.

The temporary bridge, costing nearly £3,000, opened on 27 October 1772 (in time for the annual fair two days later and less than a year after the collapse of the medieval bridge) with workmen parading through the town to musical accompaniment and with banners flying. A contemporary plan shows the bridge depended on the stump of the old where practicable: from Newcastle, traffic proceeded as far as the third pier of the medieval bridge, before veering sharply south west onto the temporary structure, built parallel to the old bridge almost as far as the last pier at the Gateshead end, where travellers returned south east back onto the roadway.

Reconstruction of the old bridge was still regarded as an option in 1773, but early in 1775 the decision was made to take down all remaining buildings on the surviving portions of the old bridge. Finally, on 5 August 1776, the Committee resolved that the entire northern part of the old bridge be dismantled and rebuilt which meant extending the temporary bridge at the northern end. By the end of 1778, Newcastle alone had spent more than £21,000 towards the permanent bridge and expected to have to find another £10,000 to complete the task. Because of the heavy outlay, authority was given in the new Act to levy tolls for a further 12 years.

The new bridge was built, on the alignment of the Roman and medieval bridges, of stone from new quarries at Elswick and St Anthony's, and for the Gateshead section from a quarry behind Oakwellgate. The foundation stone for the Bishop's section (the three southernmost arches) of the bridge was laid on 14 October 1774. By 8 July 1775 the first arch at the Gateshead end had been completed. On 25 April 1775 the first Newcastle stone was laid, by Sir Matthew White Ridley, with the sixth and final arch on the northern part completed on 13 September 1779, including the insertion of a blue boundary stone into the pavement. Again the workmen paraded through the streets, this time to a feast provided by Newcastle's Mayor. Newcastle paid for parapets along the entire length of the bridge as part of its successful attempt to persuade the Bishop not to have buildings at the Gateshead end.

With the new Tyne Bridge soon to open, the temporary bridge was sold by auction on 15 March 1781, at Kelly's Coffee House in the Sandhill, for £950 to George Stephenson.

On 28 April 1781 the Temporary Bridge closed to traffic and the following day Stephenson's workmen began to demolish it and the new stone Tyne Bridge was opened to pedestrians. Two days later wheeled traffic was permitted to cross the 91.5m long structure. The bridge was of complex construction, its varying dimensions perhaps dependent on the medieval bridge foundations, the poor quality of the river bed, and the opinions of three different engineers. Newcastle's contractors were E. Hutchinson, W. Kipling and J. Addison; the Gateshead contractors were Robert, Robert & James Shout, with J. Mylne as overseer. The new bridge, like its predecessor, carried water mains.

The trustees successfully sought another new Act in 1788, to ensure tolls for 'avenue' work on the Gateshead side, under David Stephenson's supervision. Legislation was re-enacted in 1801 extending the toll period for a further 21 years, allowing other approach works, and authorising the widening of the narrow bridge. If all borrowings for the bridge and approach works were repaid, and the repair fund continued sound within the term of this latest Act, tolls were to cease; this was achieved in 1818.

The bridge was inconveniently narrow. In October 1800 the

A detailed photograph of the Georgian Tyne Bridge, taken around 1860, a few years before its replacement.

trustees asked 'Mr Wilson of Bishopwearmouth Engineer' to prepare plans and an estimate to widen the carriageway and pavements by means of cast-iron arches sprung from the abutments. William Chapman & David Stephenson were requested to consider an alternative scheme, using stone. In their report they described Wilson's cast-iron plan design '… to be very elegant and practicable and … observe that to make it perfectly convenient to Female foot Passengers in Windy Weather, Iron Pannels should be substituted for a considerable Portion of the proposed Palisade'. They thought the bridge could be broadened by at least 1.5m on each side, but their estimate (£3,790) exceeded Wilson's (£3,092), although Stephenson would supply footpaths of 'scotch' granite 1.8m wide, with a carriageway of 6.6m, raise the bridge 61cm in the centre, and provide artificial stone parapets 1.5m high.

Stephenson undertook to maintain the additions for seven years. Newcastle, the Bishop and then the trustees approved Stephenson's plan, and obtained Parliamentary approval. He finished work in 1803, but defects were soon apparent and on examination it was reckoned that Stephenson owed the trustees £425 for uncompleted work. Between 1788 and 1819 the trustees received £1,000 per year in tolls.

Frost Fairs on the Tyne

During the 18th and 19th centuries (and probably earlier) the river Tyne was occasionally a resort for winter fun and games. In 1739 a cold snap began just after Christmas. Ice crushed and sank 12 wherries, but people adapted and the Tyne quickly resembled a fairground. Tents were set up on the ice and various sports, entertainments and trading activities took place on the frozen river over the next six weeks. From 11 February 1740 about 200 workmen were employed to create a channel through the ice above and below the bridge and the river was not completely free of ice until the end of that month.

On 7 February 1751 intense frost froze the Tyne, imprisoning a wherry between Newcastle and Gateshead. The two-man crew spent the night in sub-zero temperatures and then walked ashore across the ice into Newcastle the next morning. The Tyne was frozen for a distance of about four miles below Tyne Bridge for a few days from 14 January 1774. Several hundred people ventured onto the ice, skating and sliding. Four days later, two young men competed in a speed-skating match three miles down-river and back. Workmen were brought in soon after this to clear the ice.

On 5 January 1814 the Tyne was covered with thick ice all the way from Redheugh down to the Ouseburn. Crowds swarmed onto the ice, which was about 25.4cm thick, so deep that fires were lit on it. This may have been the winter that a bullock was roasted on the ice. There was a general carnival atmosphere, with skating and other races, football and quoits; booths were erected for the sale of liquor and cakes. There were razor grinders, musicians and even recruiting officers set up stalls. A horse pulling a sledge, and another a gig, were seen on the ice, which did not finally break up until 6 February. For some days from 6 January 1838 the river was frozen over for five miles east of Newcastle. Skaters were out in large numbers and it is said that loaded carts crossed the iced-up river during this period.

The High Level Bridge

The earliest proposal for a bridge at a high level was submitted in January 1772 by Edward Hutchinson, a Newcastle master mason. His proposed bridge was to link Pipewellgate, Gateshead, and the Javel Groupe in Newcastle, roughly on the site eventually occupied by the High Level Bridge. His 'elegant plan' was presented to the Mayor and Common Council, but only a copy of the proposal published in the *Newcastle Chronicle* survives. Hutchinson's radical idea was not to restore the old bridge on the same site, because it was too narrow at its Newcastle approach and the area around the bridge end was 'extremely offensive to passengers, who come out of the fresh air, to rush into narrow lanes at their entrance into a large town; where at first instance they breathe effluvia very disagreeable to their feelings'. A new bridge would provide a 'noble' entrance into the town, with 'a spacious street leading to the Head of the Side' and a prospect of 'that beautiful piece of architecture the steeple of St Nicholas, which is justly admired by all who have seen it'. More practical advantages of the scheme would be the complete removal of the old bridge and the extension of the Quayside for 100 yards westwards. This idea was well in advance of its time and remained on paper only.

The next proposal was by Captain Samuel Brown (1776-1852), who had designed the Union Chain Bridge at Loanend near Berwick in 1819-20 with a deck span of 118.8m. For this, he employed his invention, the wrought-iron chain link, which enabled long spans to be erected. He had proposed a suspension bridge between North and South Shields in 1825. His 1826 proposal for a similar bridge between Greene's Field, Gateshead and Back Row, Newcastle, progressed no further than surveys of the ground. A very similar scheme, designed by the Newcastle engineer William Chapman, was mentioned in 1827 by Thomas Telford, but again, without practical result. A few years later, Brown was thinking

William Martin's last proposal for a High Level Bridge, published in a leaflet of 1847. Its resemblance to Robert Stephenson's bridge is clear, although Stephenson omitted the giant lions.

along quite different lines, as his 1833 scheme for a high level crossing shows a huge cast iron arch on masonry pillars.

In 1828, an unusual project was designed by the Edinburgh lighthouse engineer Robert Stevenson, whereby a new high level bridge was to be piggy-backed on the existing Tyne Bridge. This was not built, probably because the additional structure would impose too much weight on the old bridge.

In 1836, the supremely eccentric 'Philosophical Conqueror of all Nations' William Martin, published what he claimed was his idea for a high level bridge built on top of the Tyne Bridge. Martin's designs were constantly changing as he kept up to date with other people's ideas, culminating in his 1845 design for a High Level Bridge. It was strikingly similar to that about to be built – the idea had, he said, been stolen from him by Robert Stephenson.

The next proposal was by B.R. Dodd, announced at a meeting held at the Turk's Head on 6 March, 1834. This was to be a suspension bridge from Bottle Bank to Dean Street, to 'enable carriages, passengers, and cattle to avoid the steep, difficult and dangerous hills' between the two. The scheme was revived in 1836 by Dodd and Samuel Brown, when it was claimed that a bridge would 'throw open to the vast population of Newcastle, for the purposes of health and recreation, the rides, the promenades, the beautiful scenery and salubrious air of the adjacent county of Durham'.

Soon the railway influence had begun to make itself felt and schemes to bridge the Tyne gorge multiplied. There were at least ten ideas for railway crossings between 1837 and 1845 involving such names as John and Benjamin Green, John Dobson, Richard Grainger and Isambard Kingdom Brunel. From all these schemes, Newcastle Council selected the High Level Bridge promoted by George Hudson's York, Newcastle and Berwick Railway. It was anxious that the line approaching from the south should enter the town, rather than bypass it to the east or west, so that Newcastle would form a railway hub.

The High Level Bridge was designed by Robert Stephenson and the working drawings prepared by Thomas E. Harrison, later Chief Engineer of the North Eastern Railway. It was subsequently claimed that the design was also Harrison's, but the latter corrected this view in a letter of 14 March 1846: 'The plans have been prepared under my direction: the designs are not mine, but my friend Mr Robert Stephenson's.' The bridge was a double-deck structure, the road deck being below the rail deck.

On the upper deck, there were three railway tracks supported on timber bearers resting on cast-iron cross girders. The three tracks were said later to be a compromise between the railway directors, who wanted two for cheapness, and Robert Stephenson, who preferred four to cope with increasing traffic. By the end of the century, 'the officials responsible for working the traffic would have given much to have the extra set, if not more.'

The first signs of activity appeared in October 1845, when two old houses, one on each side of the river, were whitewashed to act as site markers (they were replaced in April 1846 by scaffold poles) and demolition of properties on both sides of the river began. 650 families in Newcastle and 130 in Gateshead were displaced for the work. In the river, each of the three piers was constructed within a coffer-dam. The foundations of the piers were built of elm piles driven into the river bed by two of James Nasmyth's newly patented steam-driven pile drivers: 'The first permanent pile was driven on Thursday, Oct 1 [1846]; and notwithstanding the newness and stiffness of the machinery (which stands on a platform resting on two keels) a depth of 32 feet was attained in four minutes!' Although a few days later the keels were 'shipwrecked' and the pile driver had to be rescued from the river, the method was a great advance on hand-driving.

Meanwhile the main contracts had been let: the masonry contract for the northern approach viaducts and the river piers to Rush and Lawton of York, the southern approaches to Wilson and Gibson of Newcastle, and the bridge ironwork to Hawks, Crawshay & Sons, of Gateshead, with some of the castings being produced by Hawks' rival in Gateshead, John Abbot & Co., of Park Iron Works, and by Losh, Wilson and Bell of Walker Ironworks.

The construction method was to erect a temporary wooden bridge on the foundations of the permanent structure so the whole length of the bridge could be worked on. This apparently fragile structure could in fact carry the weight of locomotives and castings for the permanent bridge and was completed on 16 August 1848, surveyed by a government inspector on 28th and formally opened on the 29th by George Hudson. A locomotive hauling nine carriages filled with gentlemen and four ladies made the first crossing of the Tyne at a high level.

Completion of the permanent structure was rapid. The first segment of the first arch had been placed on 10 July 1848, the iron-

work was linked end to end in May 1849 and the last arch was completed on 7 June 1849. At a ceremony to mark this event, George Hawks, Mayor of Gateshead, whose family firm had completed the ironwork contract, hammered in the last key in the tension chain: 'Thus I have struck the last blow at the last arch, and crowned the labours of the skilful and industrious workmen by whom I am surrounded'. The permanent bridge was inspected by the Board of Trade representative on 11 August 1849 and tested using a train of four locomotives and 18 wagons weighing a total of 200 tons, which was thought to be 'a much greater weight in all probability than will ever pass along the bridge again'.

The first passenger train to cross the High Level was the 9.30am on 15 August and what is assumed to be the official opening was by Queen Victoria, on her way back from Scotland, on 28

September 1849. Her train stopped on the bridge while an address was read to her, but she did not leave her train (although she and the Prince Consort 'surveyed, with the greatest possible interest, the magnificent scene around and below them') and there was no formal opening ceremony. The lower roadway was not opened to the public until 5 February 1850.

In the general belt-tightening after the fall of George Hudson, the planned masonry arches at the entrances to the road deck (that at the Newcastle end to have been capped by a statue of George Stephenson) were 'deferred'. Initially, the ironwork of the bridge was painted in a stone colour (it so appears in J.W. Carmichael's famous oil painting, made before the bridge was even begun) but ten years later smoke pollution had so discoloured this that it was repainted black. For most of its life, however, it has been painted dark grey.

T.E. Harrison stated that the cost had been £491,153 (made up of: bridge, £243,096; both approaches, £113,057; land, including compensation for buildings, £135,000). The total expenditure was a vast amount for the time, although a good investment for the railway company, as the bridge has served its basic purpose until the present time. The road deck began to earn its way immediately, protected by gates and toll houses at each end. Tolls were (for example) a penny per foot passenger, threepence for a horse and wagon and 10d per 20 head of cattle. Prior to 1937, as Ken Hoole wrote, 'two grades, Toll Collector and Assistant Toll Collector, were employed on the bridge, and both were supplied with summer and winter style uniforms similar to those supplied to Ticket Collectors, but with TOLL COLLECTOR in gold on both sides of the collar.'

It was a convenient viewing platform for events on the river below, perhaps most famously the great fire. Shortly after midnight on 6 October 1854 a fire was discovered in Wilson's worsted mill in Hillgate, Gateshead. Strenuous efforts were made by firemen, soldiers and volunteers to put out the blaze but it quickly spread to adjoining buildings, including a large warehouse where metals, chemicals and inflammable goods were stored. Despite the hour, thousands turned out to watch on the quaysides and bridges. The firemen used water to attack this major conflagration. A huge explosion occurred at

J.W. Carmichael's famous painting of the High Level Bridge, completed from the designer's drawings in the early months of the construction of the bridge.

The fire of 6 October 1854, as depicted, in the Illustrated London News, *by an artist looking down from the High Level Bridge.*

Sparks and flames leapt high in the air and neighbouring properties in riverside Gateshead were engulfed. Burning debris was hurled across the Tyne, setting light to ships on the river as well as buildings on Newcastle Quayside and some streets behind, reaching even Mosley and Pilgrim Streets. Severe damage, personal injury and loss of life ensued – at least 53 dead in Gateshead and 15 in Newcastle. Such was the intensity of the blaze that some bodies were only recognisable by personal effects such as rings.

Pedestrians could not even cross the Tyne out of the rain on the new bridge, as the rail deck constantly leaked. Despite the carefully jointed planking and the felt and asphalt covering, rain cascaded down on to the wood block pavement below. This roadway, however, was in some ways ideal for the gambling fraternity of Tyneside. In 1859 a reporter for a local paper discovered that a quarter mile of straight, covered track which could be closed at both ends was ideal for dog-racing. Illustrated London News, 1 September 1849.

about 3.15am, probably caused by the reaction of the water on chemicals such as sulphur and sodium nitrate. On Gateshead Quayside 35 properties were affected, and in Newcastle 47. Fire engines and soldiers came during the course of the morning from as far away as Berwick and Carlisle to help fight the fires, which

were not finally extinguished until the next day. The total insurance loss exceeded £120,000.

The High Level also attracted exhibitionists like 'Jeffrey the Diver' (Stephen Jeffrey), who attempted to leap from the bridge into the river in 1865, having earlier made a successful leap from Monkwearmouth Bridge into the River Wear. On the High Level, he managed to avoid the police with the help of the crowd, but was eventually caught and prevented from leaping. When he was released a couple of days later, it was thought that he might try again, and police watched the bridge to forestall him, but failed to stop a total stranger, Llewellyn Gascoigne of Hartlepool, making the jump. Gascoigne survived and later appeared on the bridge to pass the hat round.

The bridge came near to destruction by fire when Robert Brown's six-story steam flour mill in the Close, near one of the Newcastle piers, burned down on 24 June 1866. The flames spread to the asphalted timber decking of the bridge and railwaymen from

Gateshead Locomotive Works tried to rip up the decking to make fire-breaks. But it was not until men from the Newcastle Naval Reserve, working from bosun's chairs slung from the bridge, managed to direct hoses onto the underside of the bridge, that the structure was saved. Only the eastern side footpath had been damaged and this was restored four days later.

The available site of Brown's mill led a few men to revive an idea which had been proposed by John and Benjamin Green in 1839, but which had been forgotten since then: a hoist from the Quayside to bridge road deck level. The three proposers of the idea were Thomas Sopwith, Addison Potter and Robert White Falconar. They obtained the necessary Act of Parliament on 12 August 1867 to operate a hoist, rather like a cliff tramway, up the eastern side of the High Level Bridge from the Close to approximately the site of the Bridge Inn, which would 'raise and lower all Persons who may offer themselves, and all Goods, Animals, Carts, Carriages, and other Articles and Things' for a toll. The capital to be raised was £4,500, but this was not forthcoming, and the hoist was never built. The idea was advocated again in 1892, but to no avail, and it was not until the new Tyne Bridge was built in 1928 that a lift from the quayside to bridge level became available.

Although street tramway services had begun in Newcastle and Gateshead in 1879 and 1884 respectively, there was no successful attempt to provide a linked service between the two systems until 1920. In October 1880 a short-lived Gateshead company had proposed to run a narrow-gauge tramway across the bridge to the Central Station, but failed to secure the approval of either the NER or Newcastle Corporation. The railway company strengthened the road deck in 1922, replacing the timber cross-girders with steel beams and providing additional suspension bolts from the inner arch ribs to the longitudinal cast iron girders carrying the roadway to support the additional loading. The tramway service across the bridge began on 10 January 1923, when a tramcar travelled from the Cloth Market, Newcastle, to Shipcote in Gateshead and back. The service was opened to the public two days later.

From about 1880 (the exact date does not appear to be on record, but the idea was possibly inspired by the failure of the scheme to run trams across the bridge) Howe Brothers of Newcastle began a service of horse-drawn brakes across the bridge at a half-penny fare (hence the 'Ha'penny Lop'). This fare was cheaper than the toll for foot passengers, so the brakes, crossing at a toll of fourpence, were very popular, and very profitable for the brake owners. There were frequent complaints about cruelty to the single horse which had to pull a bus loaded with up to 40 people, aided only by a chain (trace) horse at the start of its run across the bridge. The service ran until 12 June 1931, when a representative of the brake owners recalled to a *Weekly Chronicle* reporter that: 'we felt the effect of competition when the electric tramcars started running in 1923. I can remember when it was not difficult to get passengers but, on the other hand, we had to have policemen to keep passengers off when we had got a full load! We used to run eight buses regularly but for the last few years three have met the needs'.

Meanwhile, the structure of the bridge had been causing concern. The pier foundations had initially been enclosed in a cofferdam of timber sheet piling. The outer row had been removed in 1906, along with part of the Swing Bridge jetty, to give a wider passage between the piers for larger ships passing up-river to Armstrong's Elswick Works. In 1915, an examination by a diver found that the material underlying the concrete capping of the main piles of the pier had considerably deteriorated, sand had been replaced by mud, and the piling was out of true. Because the Tyne was in regular use by warships, no remedial action could be undertaken until after World War I. In 1919 a cofferdam was constructed

Mixed traffic on the high level Bridge, with the horse setting the pace for all. This photograph was taken on 3 June, 1924, one of a series showing the necessity for a new Tyne Bridge.

Progress was delayed by disagreements with central government (which was expected to make a grant), and it was not until 10 May 1937 that tolls were abolished. Newcastle and Gateshead Corporations paid the LNER £160,000 in compensation (much less than the £250,000 figure published in the local press) and Newcastle Corporation took over the maintenance of the road deck.

During the Second World War non-combatants at home were preparing for the better Britain which was to be created. Many government bodies, both national and local, were planning new roads and bridges and Newcastle was among them. In the 1945 Town Plan of Newcastle upon Tyne, new bridges were projected to cross the Tyne at Scotswood, Redheugh, St Anthony's and adjacent to the High Level. The new parallel bridge was intended to take northbound traffic through the city, while the existing High Level

around the south pier, and the whole foundation underpinned with concrete. The other two river piers were examined, but no faults were found.

Throughout the 1920s the road deck of the bridge was very congested and this lack of flexibility was an important factor in the building of the new Tyne Bridge. With the opening of the latter in October 1928, toll income decreased and a year later a movement began to make the High Level and the Redheugh bridges toll-free.

would carry only south-bound traffic (the Tyne and Swing bridges were to remain as they were). The new bridge was slightly west of the High Level, its approach from Wellington Street, Gateshead running under the viaduct to Gateshead West Station and thence on to the bridge. At the Newcastle end the bridge would run into Forth Street, by tunnel under the railway tracks to Westgate Road, and on to a roundabout at the foot of the Bigg Market. The road-way of the existing High Level, described as 'dismal', could be

The High Level Bridge from the Castle Keep in 1912, with the roof of the Bridge Hotel in the foreground.

treated to 'a tasteful scheme of decoration, together with a judicious siting of lamps specially spaced for the elimination of shadows'.

This was not done, and the High Level Bridge has recently celebrated its 150th birthday, having survived almost unaltered. Reduced to two rail tracks, it now carries on a daily basis only the Newcastle-Sunderland traffic, which it will lose with the extension of the Metro. The road deck is now much less busy, although it is still vital to bus links between Newcastle and the south.

The Swing Bridge

The 18th-century Tyne Bridge had a notoriously low clearance, preventing even medium-sized vessels proceeding further upstream. This meant that coal, for instance, had to be conveyed in keels (carrying about 21 tons at a time) from staiths up-river to below the bridge before transhipment into collier brigs. Similarly, goods destined for businesses above the bridge had to be unloaded at Newcastle and taken up-river in smaller boats. Armstrong's works at Elswick, which was acquiring an international reputation, was particularly inhibited from growth. Action was urgently required for the tidal reaches above the bridge.

There was perhaps more agitation about the location, width, height and design of a replacement for the 1781 Tyne Bridge than for any other Tyne crossing. In 1861 the Tyne Improvement Commission obtained Parliamentary powers to build a new opening bridge across the Tyne on the same site as previous bridges. Some Newcastle councillors felt they should have been consulted; others, including those on relevant Council committees and on the Tyne Improvement Commission, were better informed. It is hard to escape the conclusion that there was individual and collective mischief-making, possibly by vested interests. The need for a bridge less obstructive to shipping was acknowledged by everyone, except maybe the owners and crews of keels operating above bridge. By 1863, the scaremongers were claiming the new bridge would be so

This panoramic view, taken for the Tyne Improvement Commission by the pioneer photographer Thomas Worden in 1865, shows the extent to which the Georgian Tyne Bridge was a barrier to river-borne trade.

narrow that two carts would scarcely pass; in fact it was planned to be at least 2.1m wider than the existing bridge.

By May 1864 Newcastle's Tyne Bridge Approaches Committee had met with a Gateshead committee to consider several proposals: those of John Ure (the Tyne Improvement Commission engineer) for a new structure on the site of the Tyne Bridge, Richard Cail for a bridge to the west and G.T. Gibson for one to the east. Newcastle's surveyor, Thomas Bryson, reported that although Ure's plans were not fully matured, the general design and details were sufficient to show the intention. In June, Newcastle Council authorised the purchase of land for £8-9000 from Robert Brown's mill so the approach road to the new bridge could be altered. Brown had also sold property to the Tyne Improvement Commission to facilitate access to a temporary bridge between the demolition of Tyne Bridge and the completion of its successor.

By 1864, the builder and councillor Richard Cail had honed his ideas for a new bridge west of Ure's line. Cail argued that a new structure on the Tyne Bridge site would bring no lasting improvement, because the awkward approaches at each end would be perpetuated. Indeed, if his 1863 plans were accepted, there would be no need for a temporary bridge at all, producing savings of about £17,000. At a committee meeting about the removal of Tyne Bridge, most members thought Richard Cail's plan a decided improvement on the Tyne Improvement Commission proposition, although several advocated a bridge with a lifting platform to let ships through.

The Board of Trade approved Tyne Improvement Commission plans for a temporary bridge, but Newcastle's committee reported to the full Council that it had investigated Cail's idea, including measurements and costings. It recommended his solution – until the Sheriff of Newcastle, W. Lockey Harle, spoke. He regretted that after three years of discussion and deliberation, vigorous attempts

 ## A first Tyne Tunnel?

A tunnel was one of the many ideas put forward to replace the old Tyne Bridge and solve the navigational problem. This was clearly a serious proposal, for dimensions and route are given on a Tyne Improvement Commission plan of 1864: it was to be 3m in height, and run for 173.8m at a gradient of 1 in 57, at a depth of 12.2m below the river bed on the Newcastle side to 9.1m on the Gateshead side; it was to start just behind the entrance to the Tyne Bridge at Newcastle and run south-west to a point below the Gateshead end of the High Level Bridge.

were being made to reverse a previous committee's decisions, reached after extensive consideration of the plans and ideas of Ure, Gibson, Cail, and Bryson. The earlier committee had realised Cail's proposal was impractical, as a swing bridge to the west would actually hit the High Level Bridge as it turned! Lockey Harle stressed that matters were best left to the Tyne Improvement Commission, also pointing out that a temporary bridge would cost £8-9000; half the cost of this would be recouped by the eventual sale of its timber and other materials, while the other half would be redeemed by using the temporary bridge for the construction of the Swing Bridge.

At this stage, statistics and census results were used to support differing viewpoints. Swing bridge opponents said people would be inconvenienced. John Ure estimated a traffic stoppage of less than ten minutes each time a ship passed through, but Newcastle's committee reckoned the delay would be about 15 minutes, with pedestrians and vehicles delayed, and jostling occurring when the bridge closed, worsening on market days and doubtless

Traffic census, 1859 and 1864

The police were asked to conduct a census of traffic over the old Tyne Bridge and the High Level Bridge.

Between Saturday 24 and Tuesday 27 December 1864, 3,461 vehicles crossed the Tyne Bridge and 1,755 the High Level. On market day, Tuesday 31 January 1865, a total (both directions) of 18,414 persons crossed the Tyne Bridge in 12 hours. The Tyne Improvement Commission's own calculations, collected over six days (Monday-Saturday) in August 1859 were (in both directions):

	foot,	carts,	carriages,	wagons,	horsemen,	livestock
Tyne Bridge:	168,098;	7,778;	659;	366;	718;	3,481
High Level:	27,268;	2,363;	1,054;	140;	425;	888

That same August the Tyne Improvement Commission assessed the number of keels and steamboats navigating the river above the Tyne Bridge over 12 days:

	Laden, up;	Laden, down;	Light, up;	Light down
Keels :	378;	1094;	1180;	348

Steamboats (up): 82; (down) 80.

All told, about 800 tons of goods were brought down to the Tyne Bridge daily.

deteriorating further in the future as traffic increased. The committee, to prove their point, researched the situation at other swing bridges, such as Hull and Liverpool, unsurprisingly finding traffic was greatly inconvenienced at both. One possible alternative was to remove the Tyne Bridge and have everyone cross by the High Level, but this would involve reactivating tolls that had ceased 50 years before. (The engineer, T.E. Harrison, stated that the High Level Bridge would be totally inadequate to carry all cross-river traffic.) Some committee members chased wild ideas, such as a moving platform operating at night, while the more responsible realised there was no real alternative to the Tyne Improvement Commission scheme.

Although recognising that most 'foot passengers' wanted a low-level crossing, Newcastle also considered constructing another high-level bridge. This would cost £14,500 to purchase land and another £40-50,000 to build. To remove awkward approaches, a new bridge from the foot of Dean Street would cost more, £25,000 to buy up property, and £150,000 for materials and construction!

Newcastle and Gateshead Councils' Joint Committee interviewed a series of witnesses before attempting to make up its mind. John Ure admitted the keel trade would disappear if a swing bridge was built. His view was confirmed by the harbourmaster, who stated that collier brigs would be able to get direct to the coal spouts upstream if a swinging bridge was built and the river deepened as far as Blaydon and Stella – a great improvement for colliery-owners and industry generally. Ure reiterated that bridge opening and closing, with the time a ship took to pass through, would be about six minutes – more allowing for winds and tides or a larger vessel. A screw steamer would be quicker, and one vessel could pass through each way simultaneously. Asked about mechanical breakdown, potentially blocking both land and river traffic, Ure declared that as it was a hydraulic system this would not happen. He added that the Tyne Improvement Commission had spent over £250,000 on dredgers to deepen the river above and below the bridge, had bought land for the swing bridge approaches, and was buying plant to construct bridge foundations; the overall scheme would open up the river and reduce flooding. The advantages greatly exceeded the apparent high cost.

When the scheme was complete he expected sailing vessels up

to 400 tons and screw/paddle steamers up to 1,200 tons to be able to proceed to the navigable limit of Hedwin Streams. Just when Ure appeared to have dealt with all the arguments, a steam ferry was suggested instead of a bridge. Another councillor urged a two-year postponement, but Ure needed dredgers up-river as soon as possible, and this could not happen until the Tyne Bridge was demolished.

Two months later, Newcastle's Tyne Bridge Approaches Committee, still undecided, debated the merits of swing, draw, lifting, and high-level bridges. But the necessary legislation had by this time been approved by Parliament.

The temporary timber bridge used during the construction of the Swing Bridge, 1875.

Locally, the Sheriff's intervention, and probably the supremacy of the Tyne Improvement Commission scheme, brought bickering to an end at last. By 6 March 1867, the Tyne Improvement Commission had completed its initial dredging and improvement works up to the 18th-century Tyne Bridge and had finalised the swing bridge plans, which were then presented to the Board of Trade, and Newcastle and Gateshead Councils, for approval.

A temporary bridge was erected in 1865-1866 so the Tyne Bridge could be dismantled, and the foundations and machinery for its successor built. In addition, the temporary bridge had a gangway on its east side to carry steam and air pipes and materials from the work yard in Gateshead during the construction of the Swing

Bridge. The temporary bridge was opened without ceremony on 17 September 1866, in the presence of several Tyne Improvement Commission members, and cost £14,236 to build. It was evidently erected so dredging equipment could pass up and downstream without hindrance. During its ten-year life it carried a heavy volume as well as weight of traffic (on one occasion a 50-ton steam boiler on a carriage drawn by 20 horses).

Once the temporary bridge was in place, workmen began to demolish the Tyne Bridge. By the summer of 1867 parts of nine arches and eight piers had been partially removed; on 12 February 1872 the blue stone was taken out, and the stumps of four piers were left to support scaffolding and aid in the building of the new

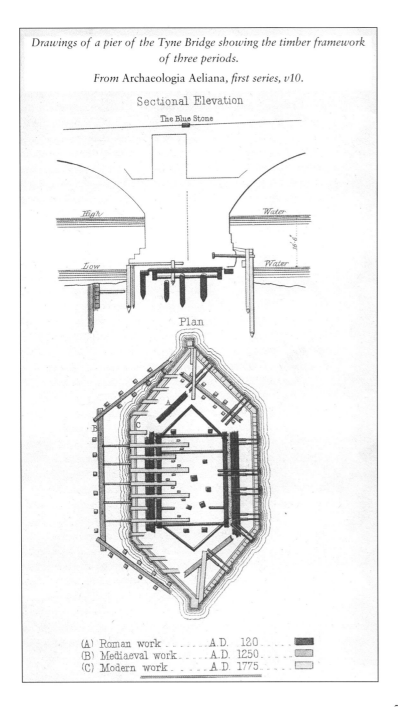

Drawings of a pier of the Tyne Bridge showing the timber framework of three periods.

From Archaeologia Aeliana, *first series, v10.*

Sectional Elevation

The Blue Stone

High   Water

Low   Water

16'-6"

Plan

A

B   C

(A) Roman work . . . . A.D. 120 . . . . .
(B) Mediaeval work . . . . A.D. 1250 . . . . .
(C) Modern work . . . . . A.D. 1775 . . . . .

bridge. During this dismantling, an interesting discovery was made: 'On the removal of the third pier from the Gateshead side, the one which … carried the blue stone, a curious sight presented itself, the foundations of all the three bridges were to be seen. The medieval builders had made use of the work of the Romans … and the builders of 1775 [*sic*] had availed themselves of the labours of both … Piles had been driven … by the builders of all the bridges, and a timber framework constructed corresponding to the size and form of the pier … In all … three bridges the form of the piers was the same … a cut-water up and down the stream, but they … differed in size. The Roman was the smallest, allowing for a roadway of about [5.5m] 18 feet … the usual width of their military ways. The medieval was the widest, and would thus give the greatest resistance to the passage of the waters. The structure of the framework was different … the Gateshead side of the pier was different from that of the Newcastle side … There was a difference in the timber of the three bridges. The Roman oak was black, friable on the outside but solid in the heart. The medieval was of a brown colour somewhat decayed on the outside but firm within. The timber of the last century was quite fresh and new-looking. The superintendent of the workmen considered that the carpentry of the Roman framework was superior to that of the two others'.

Building of the Swing Bridge began on 23 September 1868. The three piers of solid masonry, like the stone abutments, were constructed under the supervision of John Ure and his colleague and successor, Philip Messent, and were all founded on concrete-filled cast-iron caissons sunk down to bedrock about 13.7m below low water. The bridge spans four river channels, spaced so the piers coincide with those of the High Level Bridge (as recommended by an earlier engineer, W.A. Brooks, in 1854). Services for the bridge are carried via this larger neighbour. The wrought-iron superstructure of bowstring girders and the sophisticated machinery were manufactured and fitted by W.G. Armstrong's, the foremost builders of swing bridges, at their Elswick works. Some ironwork was unfortunately so distorted in a fire there that it had to be replaced.

Even allowing for the Elswick fire, it is strange that Armstrong's took so long to make and fit the innovative new bridge since the firm stood to gain so much from its existence. As it was, the Swing Bridge was opened to vehicular and pedestrian traffic without ceremony (possibly because it still lacked finishing touches) on 25 June 1876. Three weeks later the first swing was made to allow a ship to pass through. This first vessel was (appropriately for the Roman bridge site) the Italian naval transport *Europa*, which proceeded through on 17 July on its way to Elswick to load a 100-ton Armstrong gun, at that time the largest piece of ordnance ever manufactured. The difference that the Swing Bridge made was colossal, for the Durham coalfield, for Armstrong's (markedly so from 1883 when Elswick Shipyard opened), for the lead works of Walkers, Parker, and for several firebrick and pipe factories, and other firms.

The two central openings of the Swing Bridge each provide a passage for shipping 31.7m wide, spanned by the swinging superstructure based on the central pier. Despite the weight (1,450 tons) of this moveable portion of the bridge, it turns (almost always in an anti-clockwise direction, following vessels round) 90 degrees in as many seconds, with no apparent difficulty. The swinging superstructure is supported at its centre on a ring of rollers resembling a

The construction of the Swing Bridge goes forward with the stumps of the Georgian Tyne Bridge piers still in place.

gun turret's mechanism. All the bridge machinery is housed in the sub-structure of the central pier, while the control floor is located in a cupola mounted over the roadway. The working method depends upon the generation and storage of water under pressure, which is then used to power the engines that turn the bridge.

The bridge was designed to carry a rolling load up to 60 tons mounted on four wheels; down to 1924 the heaviest load recorded was a traction engine pulling a trailer carrying a 59-ton boiler. Clearance is 3.1m above high water when the bridge is closed.

A busy Swing Bridge in June 1924, with traffic starting to cross after an opening.

When completed it was the largest swing bridge built, and had cost around £240,000. To that has to be added the cost of erecting and removing the temporary bridge (£14,236), demolishing the Tyne Bridge (£11,516), land purchases and compensation (£22,510), making the final figure not far short of £300,000.

By 1878 there were complaints about the time it took to get the bridge open: '[a] ship had to wait because Mr Brown [the Bridge Master] was at his dinner. It was a large vessel of upwards of 2,000 tons, drawing [6.1m] 20 feet of water, and it had to wait until Mr Brown came from his dinner'. Actually, the machinery to open the

The Swing Bridge opens in about 1920 to allow a Tyne Improvement Commission paddle tug and dredger through.

bridge took 45 minutes to get up steam! The regulations were then revised so that ships' captains gave sufficient notice. By 1890 four hours notice was required, with the bridge opening no more than 15 minutes at a time during normal working hours, and not at all in stormy or foggy weather or when the river was in flood. Ten

minutes before opening a steam whistle would blow three times, and before the bridge swung open a bell would sound continuously.

The Tyne Improvement Act of 1864 authorised the use of the 1801 trust fund, established to maintain the Georgian Tyne Bridge, for the Swing Bridge (except superstructure and machinery). By

The Swing Bridge closing after the passage up-river of a cargo ship.

steam boilers were replaced after 47 years of continuous service. The swinging centre-span is operated hydraulically; for many years this machinery was steam-driven but in 1959 it was converted to an electrically-powered system. This apart, most of the original design features are still in working order today.

About 300,000 ships have passed through the Swing Bridge since 1876; in its peak year, 1924, around 6,000 vessels (about 20 a day) passed the Bridge, mostly colliers to and from the coal staiths (connected by rail to the Durham pits) up-river; by 1927 the largest vessel recorded through the Swing Bridge was HMS *Canada* of 32,000 tons, although it was by no means uncommon for ships drawing around 9.1m of water to pass through. By the 1970s numbers were down to about 900 and in 2000 the bridge was opened just 39 times. The Swing Bridge, now a listed building, is probably the most important surviving hydraulic turning bridge in this country – perhaps anywhere – and the fact that it is still in operation so close to its place of manufacture makes it of special local interest. It may no longer be in frequent use, but is manned 24 hours a day, 365 days a year.

The old blue stone is preserved in the Castle Keep.

1888 the original £1,000 had grown to almost £12,000. Newcastle and the Tyne Improvement Commission were prepared to promote a parliamentary Bill transferring all the original repair funds from Newcastle and the Ecclesiastical Commissioners (who had inherited from the Bishop of Durham) to the Tyne Improvement Commission; however, the Tyne Improvement Commission was not prepared to relieve the other two parties of all responsibility, and the proposal consequently collapsed, to be renewed later, again without progress. In 1888 the Tyne Improvement Commission resurfaced the roadway, with Newcastle paying for this out of the fund. From 1890 to 1924 repairs cost just £8,160. However, in 1922 the girders on the swinging portion of the bridge had to be renewed (by Armstrong's), and the wood paving re-blocked. In 1923 the two

The Redheugh Ferry and Bridges

Redheugh Ferry

This was one of the small 'Direct' ferries that once plied across the Tyne. It probably came into being to assist workmen to reach the opposite shore quickly, as industry developed on both sides of the river. The Redheugh ferry ran on a line west of Redheugh bridge, crossing from the lead works on the Newcastle side to Redheugh. It was operating by 1846 and continued into the 20th century

The First Redheugh Bridge

The concept of a bridge connecting the western outskirts of Newcastle and Gateshead had been discussed since the 1830s. The earliest proposal was for a road and rail bridge between Elswick Colliery and Askew's Quay, Gateshead (the site of the future Newcastle and Carlisle Station) in 1830. A year later a railway bridge was suggested, but neither of these ideas was acted upon.

Almost 30 years later a proposal was put forward by the contractor and builder Richard Cail to build a rail/road bridge at Redheugh. The rail deck was to be below the road (a reversal of the High Level Bridge idea) carrying the main north-south line through the Team Valley into Newcastle Central Station without the need for trains to reverse. But this excellent concept did not meet with the approval of Thomas Elliot Harrison, the NER Company's engineer (who had his own plans and proposals in 1865) and so never happened, though Harrison admitted that another bridge across the Tyne would eventually be needed by the railway.

Despite the NER's non-participation, Cail and others went ahead with a road-only bridge, forming the Redheugh Bridge and Approaches Company in October 1865. Without the NER the proposals were necessarily modest, with an authorised capital of only £40,000 with power to borrow a further £13,000, a total of £53,000. Bridge income was to be derived from tolls.

Initially, the directors of the company were chiefly businessmen with interests in the development of the Redheugh area. Joseph Watson and his son, Robert Spence Watson, the solicitors, were included, the latter as company secretary. The company's minutes show that only a minority of these directors took any deep interest in it; there were rarely more than three present at meetings. One of the directors, R.S. Newall, a wire-rope manufacturer, ensured that a commitment was entered in the company's minutes to buy any supplies of wire rope from his firm.

In October 1866 the bridge company contacted the local water and gas companies to invite them to make use of the bridge for a fee, but instead both the Newcastle and Gateshead Water Company and the Newcastle and Gateshead Gas Company subscribed £5,000 in shares to enable them to run their mains across the bridge. A further large shareholding of £10,000 was taken by the Askew family, owners of Redheugh Estate, in the expectation that their land would increase in value after the bridge was built. In addition to the family shareholding, Henry Askew gave a further £20,000 to get the work started. Thus three quarters of the company's modest capital requirements was raised from three sources, though initially it proved difficult to find other subscribers.

The Royal Assent to the Act of Parliament was granted on 11 June 1866, tenders for the bridge sought in December 1867, and work began in July 1868. The engineer chosen to design the bridge was Thomas Bouch. His Redheugh Bridge was a slender construction with three river piers, each comprising four cylinders filled with concrete, carrying four columns, horizontally and diagonally braced, which extended 20.5m above the roadway. The main trough girders supporting the roadway also carried the water pipes, while the top girders were circular iron tubes, one of which, on the eastern side of the bridge, was the gas main. The roadway was 6.1m wide (identical to the High Level) with a 2.1m pathway cantilevered out on either side.

The masonry of the bridge was by Walter Scott, who suffered an early disappointment when the arch nearest the river on the north bank partially collapsed due to the instability of the sand, and had to be repaired. The sand 'boiling up' also caused problems to the men constructing the piers. The ironwork was contracted for by Thomas William Panton & Sons of Sunderland, who had built bridges for the NER, but who went bankrupt in December 1869. These delays were exacerbated because insufficient men were employed in construction. The resident engineer, Mr Gibson, constantly complained to the board of directors about the slow progress of the work. In some weeks, as few as 17 men were working on the actual bridge. Mr Tillotson, in charge of the ironwork, was firmly told in September 1870 that if he did not use more men the bridge company would employ them at his expense: this appears to have done the trick. There were also delays in delivery of materials due to the bad state of the roads, especially Askew Road, where carters found it impossible at times to get their horses and wagons through the mud.

Even nature was unkind to the Redheugh Bridge. On 7 January 1871, as it neared completion, drifting ice on the river carried all the scaffolding of the large span at the Newcastle end out to sea and it was lost. But by the middle of the year, ornamental ends to the main girders, made by Hawks, Crawshay, had been fixed, lamp standards erected on the bridge, the toll houses painted, papered and tenanted. The Redheugh Bridge was opened for pedestrians on 1 May 1871 and for wheeled traffic a month later, although the timber guards to the river piers were not completed until October.

Though cheaply built, the Redheugh Bridge lasted quite well,

possibly due to the light loadings it carried. Financially, however, the bridge was not the instant success which had been hoped for; there was no dividend paid until 1873 and the directors took no fees until 1884. Part of the reason for the initial lack of custom was the primitive nature of the southern approach roads, which the company could not persuade Gateshead Corporation to take over and maintain. The bridge was 'in a sense, rather before its time', being completed some years before the population had grown enough to make it economical. By the close of the 1870s, however, much of the land in the Redheugh/Teams areas had been sold for housing, and the bridge began to pay reasonable dividends. In 1875 the tolls were let for £3,000 per annum; in 1878 for £4,520.

The company had various ideas for adding to its revenue: for example, they charged spectators sixpence to watch HMS *Victoria* pass under the bridge on its way down-river from Armstrong, Mitchell's Elswick yard in 1887. It was customary to charge a fee of twopence or threepence to watch a sculling race from such an excellent vantage point. Less welcome were the beggars who plagued the bridge (sometimes as many as five at a time) until they were banned in 1896.

In 1889 the bridge was inspected by Sir John Fowler and his colleague, Benjamin Baker, designers of the Forth railway bridge. They presented their report to the directors on 23 October. It was generally favourable, although they did point out that all four columns in the centre pier were 'more or less cracked' and that the large capping stone 2.4m in diameter and 0.6m thick, which carried the iron columns supporting the bridge structure, was fractured in several places.

Doubts persisted, however, and in October 1892, aged 80 and with only a year to live, Richard Cail, now chairman and managing director of the Redheugh Bridge Company, published a pamphlet in support of the bridge, emphasising its basic strength. When Cail

The first Redheugh Bridge in 1876. In the far distance, beyond the High Level Bridge, the temporary Tyne Bridge can be glimpsed.

died his brother was appointed company chairman in his place and J. Watt Sandeman of Newcastle, engineer, was asked to survey the bridge. Sandeman's report said of the piers 'so far as could be seen, everything was in order'. In 1895 Sandeman conducted a more thorough, six-week inspection and discovered: 'The examination of the cross-girders has revealed a very serious state of corrosion and damage and defective workmanship.' Repairs were estimated at £22,815, including 'the constructive difficulties to be surmounted in strengthening an old structure of this character [involve] greater trouble than would be incurred in the design of a new bridge'. A

second engineer's opinion was sought from A.J. Barry who also advocated a new bridge and indeed submitted a plan of his own for the rebuilding. Sandeman and his partner, Moncrieff's, proposed new bridge would cost £63,800. Coal was likely to be worked under the bridge so a series of separate truss girders for each span was advisable.

The directors reluctantly decided that they would have to bite the bullet and build a new bridge rather than patch up the old one. All the components of the bridge, which was to be constructed of mild steel, were to be rigorously tested before assembly. Particular attention was paid to the rivets, which were to be of ingot steel, not scrap steel.

The Second Redheugh Bridge

The gas and water companies again agreed to subscribe £5,000 each and also contribute £3,500 each towards costs. Sandeman and Moncrieff drew up plans and Sir Benjamin Baker was appointed consulting engineer. Sir William Arrol's tender for £72,411 was accepted with an agreed time of two years from commencement to completion. Arrol's had a substantial reputation as bridge builders: they had constructed the the Forth Railway Bridge (1883-90) and Tower Bridge, London (1886-94) among other structures, but they were a sad disappointment to the Redheugh Bridge Company and its engineers. The saga of the first bridge was repeated, with delays

in preparing materials in Glasgow and the employment of too few men on site. 1897 dragged into early 1900 with no sign of completion.

In March 1900 Sandeman and Moncrieff wrote despairingly to Arrol's 'We have so often verbally protested against the delay without effect that we feel it is useless to do more than put these facts on record.' However, later the same year work speeded up, despite some local problems when the engineers reported that 'Messrs Arrols have had difficulty in obtaining men of sufficiently good class in the neighbourhood, and they have consequently promised to send a gang of erectors from Glasgow'.

By October 1900 the erection of the main truss girders of all four spans was complete; they were built out as cantilevers from each of the three river piers simultaneously, enclosing the old bridge

Redheugh Bridge in 1898, looking from the Newcastle side, with work barely begun on its reconstruction. In the foreground, a flock of sheep is about to cross to market.

structure, the movement being by means of hydraulic jacks. By mid-1901 it was time to substitute the new bridge for the old and *The Engineer* reported: 'This exceptional and remarkable operation was performed on 6th May [1901], the early dawn being selected, so that there should be as little disturbance as possible from spectators. Eight hydraulic jacks were employed, one at each end of the four spans. The total weight moved was about 1,600 tons. The spans rested on well-greased rails, and the gas and water mains were, of course, disconnected. The rams used were [23cm] 9in diameter with short stroke.'

The jacks moved the whole of the bridge superstructure 1.4m to the west until it rested on the new piers. The gas and water mains were then reconnected and the structure of the old bridge removed. The final cost to the company was £77,482, which was raised by calls on shareholders, loans, and mortgages on the tolls. The bridge was opened on 13 August 1901, but did not remain problem-free for long. In May 1906 J.M. Moncrieff, the company's engineer, reported that the Gateshead end of the bridge had begun to slip laterally eastwards. By May 1909, the total slippage was 7.6cm. The workings of the Redheugh Coal Company, which underlay the south abutment, were suspected (the Bridge Company had paid compensation to the colliery company in 1900 on condition that they left additional pillars

In March 1901 the spans of the second Redheugh Bridge were in the process of being moved into place.

of coal to support the bridge and its approaches) but this was never proved. Moncrieff planned to reconstruct both bridge approaches at a cost of £35,000, but luckily for the company's purse, the movement stopped. A timber trestle was added at the Gateshead end to support the two steel girders. In 1922 this was replaced in steel and tie-rods fixed to concrete blocks in the roadway. Toll revenue, which had been high during the war, was decreasing due to the post-war trade depression. In December 1922 about 40 hunger marchers crossed from Gateshead to Newcastle without paying the toll

demanded by the helpless tollkeepers.

The 1920s saw a period of great expansion in bus services, both local and long distance, and the company began to profit greatly from the bridge's position as the only alternative to the congested High Level. Although the buses gave the company some anxious moments by speeding across the bridge at anything up to 28 mph (the limit was 6mph, increased in 1928 to 10mph), this source of revenue became increasingly valuable. The opening, in October 1928, of the toll-free Tyne Bridge was bad news for the company. In

The Newcastle end of the Redheugh Bridge in 1965, with the speed and weight restrictions prominently displayed.

of £151,000 for Redheugh Bridge. The directors recommended immediate acceptance, meanwhile reducing their own tolls by 25 per cent from April 1929.

Traffic censuses taken in 1928 and 1930 showed a 25 per cent drop in motor traffic, despite the lower tolls, confirming the directors in their view that the company had no viable future. Meanwhile there was considerable delay on the Corporations' purchase of the bridge and problems for the company multiplied. In 1931, Gateshead Corporation threatened to close Mulgrave Terrace and Askew Road to bus traffic; the newly established Traffic Commissioners routed more buses over the High Level; and the bridge's engineer stated that it was not strong enough to carry the new double-decker buses.

In 1934 the question of selling the bridge arose again and the bridge was finally bought by Gateshead and Newcastle Corporations on 10 May 1937 and tolls abolished. After the war, the limitations of the Redheugh Bridge were more evident. Although no tolls were received, the Corporation still had to pay for watchmen at each end to ensure that vehicles did not exceed the eight-ton weight limit; this, and the overall strength of the bridge 'leave no doubt as to the necessity of the bridge being rebuilt.' Both approaches were to be improved, especially the north, which was to begin at Scotswood Road, run over Railway Street and the Forth goods sidings at a level six feet higher than the old bridge and thence across the river to Gateshead. But the Redheugh Bridge had many more years of life as the economy, weakened by the war and its aftermath, could not afford major

February 1929 the London and North Eastern Railway (LNER) announced their intention to operate buses across the High Level free of toll. Newcastle and Gateshead Corporations made an offer

capital projects. An engineers' report in 1964 stated that if the bridge was to be retained beyond 1970 a major reconstruction of its approaches would be necessary; further, it had poor load and traffic capacity as well as an 'unsure structural condition'.

The Third Redheugh Bridge

First considered in 1949 to replace its deteriorating predecessor, the initial design was announced in 1967: a box-girder bridge to be opened in 1971, at a cost of £4.75 million. After much delay, as well as planning alterations on the approaches, the design was changed to a reinforced concrete bridge.

The present Redheugh Bridge was designed by Mott, Hay, and Anderson (now Mott MacDonald) to a brief prepared by Tyne and Wear County Council. The architects were Holford Associates. The main contractor was Edmund Nuttall Ltd. in association with its Dutch parent company, HBM bv and 19 sub-contractors. Work commenced on 24 April 1980, on a site about 25m downstream from the old bridge.

This new high-level link between Newcastle and Gateshead is of pre-stressed, post-tensioned concrete box construction. The twin-cells of the bridge contain a water main and two gas mains displaced from the old bridge, together with telephone and electricity cables. The cellular construction allows for regular and convenient inspection of both bridge condition and the services below the roadway. Small portholes are provided at frequent intervals in the walls and floor of the box system to ventilate cavities and prevent gas concentration and possible explosion in the event of a leak. The designers specified high-

Mott MacDonald

The new Redheugh Bridge takes shape next to the old.

strength steel, together with double-thickness waterproofing under the asphalt carriageway, to guard against possible damage by common salt used for ice and snow clearance, which might otherwise attack the steel reinforcements in the concrete.

As the most westerly of the Newcastle bridges, the Redheugh receives the full force of the prevailing wind blowing down the Tyne valley. For this reason a guardrail was built at the edge of the footpath. In addition, parapets were provided at frequent intervals to contain vehicles. Nevertheless, there have been near misses, including a double-decker bus, despite the speed restrictions imposed when high winds have threatened the stability of vehicles on the bridge.

The present Redheugh road bridge was opened to vehicular traffic a month ahead of schedule, on Monday, 21 February 1983. The official opening was by the Princess of Wales, on Wednesday, 18 May 1983. The cost of the new structure was just over £15 million, which included nearly £11 million for civil engineering and construction, and £2 million for the demolition of the old Redheugh bridge.

The revisers of Nikolaus Pevsner, writing before the Millennium Bridge was conceived, described this structure as 'The most striking of the new Tyne bridges and a good example of modern medium-span design'.

Mott MacDonald

The elegant lines of the completed Redheugh Bridge.

King Edward VII Bridge

The 'new High Level' was built for, and entirely financed by, the NER. It was desperately needed to supplement the 50-year old High Level Bridge, whose three tracks carried about 800 train and light engine movements every day – all the main north-south traffic together with local traffic to South Shields and Sunderland. The problem had long been recognised by the company and a new high level bridge on an almost identical site had been suggested by Thomas Elliot Harrison in 1865, when the present main line was being planned through the Team Valley.

In 1893, while the NER was doubling the width of the Dean Street Bridge, it decided to consider the problem of the river crossing as part of a review of its activities in and around Newcastle. They asked Sir John Wolfe Barry to prepare schemes and estimates. Among his ideas were: widening the High Level Bridge to six tracks; reconsidering T.E. Harrison's 1865 scheme; realigning the Team Valley main line to cross the Tyne by a new bridge from near Dunston Staiths to join the Newcastle and Carlisle line at Elswick; a new river crossing below

Newcastle between Pelaw and Heaton. All these ideas raised objections from the NER directors, and no more was heard of them, except the last, which resurfaced in 1918. From the railway company's point of view, a new bridge would give Newcastle Central Station a through-running facility for mainline north-south trains, avoiding the reversing manoeuvre necessary with only a single river crossing. A mere widening of the High Level would not have solved this problem.

A span of the King Edward VII Bridge emerges from a clutter of timber scaffolding, 10 May 1905.

A contemporary photograph of a drawing of the longitudinal section of the North Pier caisson of the King Edward VII Bridge, showing excavators working at the bottom under compressed air.

piers almost on the banks, so that navigation was little interfered with. These plans changed hardly at all, but the many borings into the river bed to discover footings for the piers caused long delays. Despite the fact that the Redheugh Bridge rebuilding was taking place less than 91.4m up-river and the results of their borings were shared with the railway company, the latter's engineers undertook two series of borings 18 months apart, the second series being completed in early 1902. Even so, it was discovered only during the excavations for the bridge foundations on the south side of the river that the rock strata was too badly fissured to support the proposed girder span, which was replaced by a series of stone arches.

The three 'river' piers were built on caissons, as opposed to the piles driven into the river bed to support the original High Level Bridge. At that time the Tyne had been not much more than 90cm deep where the bridge was to be built, but 50 years later constant dredging to provide a deep channel up-river to Armstrong's Elswick Works had made this method impossible. Each caisson was a mild steel construction weighing 667 tons (the largest used by this date) with a cutting edge and, as they sank, labourers excavated the silt, gravel, clay and soft coal. A total of 150 men worked in the caissons under compressed air. No one over the age of 40 could be

Parliamentary powers to build the bridge were not obtained until 1899. It was designed by Charles Augustus Harrison, Chief Engineer of the northern division of the NER and nephew of Thomas Elliot Harrison of High Level Bridge fame. The contract was let on 6 March 1902 to the Cleveland Bridge and Engineering Company of Darlington and on 29 July Harrison laid the foundation stone at the north end of the bridge.

When the plans were published in the local press in 1898, the central pier was in the centre of the river, and the other two 'river'

employed and the men spent a maximum of four hours in the caissons. Nevertheless, one man died and one was seriously ill partly as a result of working in compressed air. 'Generally speaking, small wiry men are found most suitable for the work'. Some of the excavators became ill through breathing in sulphuretted hydrogen emanating from the coal seams they passed through.

When sunk to the rock, the caissons were filled with concrete up to riverbed level. These supported the Norwegian granite piers which carried the deck. The approach viaducts on either side were built of hard red sandstone from Dumfriesshire. The Act of Parliament under which the bridge was constructed allowed the contractors to close half the navigable waterway for temporary periods, so that the girders could be erected using staging in the river.

A group of divers with their apparatus, June 1905.

The construction was finished without major incident and the result was a highly efficient, though extremely heavy, railway bridge. Although not fully complete, the bridge was opened by King Edward VII on 10 July 1906 from a temporary platform at the southern end of the bridge. On 27 September the 'girders were tested by the Board of Trade with a live load of ten locomotives, coupled together in two sets of five each. At a given signal the two sets of locomotives travelled side by side over the bridge at a speed of between six and eight miles per hour, one set passing over the track on the east side of the girder to be tested and the other on the west side of the same girder.' The ten locomotives averaged 100 tons each in weight. The bridge was fully opened for traffic on 1 October. The cost (exclusive of land) was £500,000 and it was described as Britain's last great railway bridge.

The King Edward VII bridge on 7 September 1905. A remarkable aid to construction was the cableway across the river, which, it was estimated, carried over 23,000 tons of materials. The largest such cableway in the world, it had a main steel cable 7.6cm in diameter and 463.5m long, suspended 61m above high water. When dismantled in 1906, the main cable was sent down the Tyne to Swan Hunter & Wigham Richardson, where it was used in the launch of the Mauretania.

King Edward VII Bridge, over 70 years after opening, through the girders of the old and new Redheugh Bridges.

The Tyne Bridge was opened on 10 October 1928 by King George V and Queen Mary. Intrepid spectators watched from nearby rooftops.

The Tyne Bridge of 1928

Although briefly considered in 1864 during the discussions of a replacement for the Georgian Tyne bridge, the idea for a new bridge at a high level was first seriously mooted in 1883. It was felt by a majority of members of Newcastle Town Council that the NER was profiting far too much from the tolls imposed on traffic across the road deck of the High Level Bridge. The NER and others thought that those who took the commercial risk should garner the profits. Others held that there had been a longstanding agreement that the railway company should give up its right to tolls once initial outlay had been recouped. Unfortunately, this supposed agreement had been a verbal one, and no written record could be found.

In 1883 it was proposed that the Newcastle and Gateshead town councils should unite to construct the new bridge from High Street, Gateshead to Pilgrim Street, Newcastle, at an estimated cost of £200,000, excluding land. If necessary, construction could be partly funded by levying a toll on the new bridge. The experienced builder and contractor Alderman Richard Cail, who had built the railway viaduct at Durham, thought that 'Bridge building was comparatively in its infancy at the time that the High Level bridge was built; and bridges could now be built expeditiously and at less cost'. Later in the year, the two councils took a traffic survey which appeared to show that 85,000 people crossed the bridge each week and that tolls on a new bridge would produce about £14,000 a year. The construction cost of £200,000 was to be divided, two thirds to Newcastle and one third to Gateshead.

The site for the bridge was to be east of the High Level Bridge, near the Swing Bridge. The roadway was to be the same height above the water as the lower deck of the High Level, but more than double the width at 15.2m. A single span steel arch was proposed, on stone columns, with four arches on each side. The Newcastle approach was to begin near the Moot Hall, and one of the support pillars was to be on the site of the Fish Market (opened in 1880), which would have to be demolished. At its Gateshead end, the approach would be along Hill Street or Half Moon Lane, curving into High Street.

There was silence for nine years, until a similar plan was proposed in July 1892. This time, in addition to the complaint about the High Level Bridge tolls, it was argued that that a new bridge would ease traffic problems in Blackett and Grainger Streets and improve tramway links. The inevitable committee was formed, meeting intermittently over the next few years, initially considering a joint bridge with the NER, then coming out in favour of working with Gateshead Council only. The latter then proposed the two Councils should attempt to buy the Redheugh Bridge, the owners of which were promoting a bill in Parliament for its reconstruction. Another special committee was formed which would consider all possible variants. In May 1897, after several meetings with the Gateshead Committee, a report was presented to Newcastle City Council recommending that the two authorities should build a new bridge from High Street to Pilgrim Street of sufficient strength to carry two lines of tramway and financed by tolls.

What was proposed at this period was a cantilever bridge, supported by a single pier on each quayside, with the same river clearance as the High Level Bridge. The roadway was to be 10m wide, with two 3m footpaths at either side. There was to be a hydraulic lift for foot-passengers from quayside to bridge level on the Newcastle side, and possibly a lift for road vehicles.

In March 1900, a short but emphatic letter from the Town Clerk of Gateshead informed the Newcastle committee that 'the time has not arrived for the erection by the two Corporations of a new High Level Bridge'. The main reason for Gateshead's reluctance was the cost which, though much less than Newcastle's, would have borne heavily on a borough with a very low rateable value. And so it remained for over two decades: though committees continued to meet, no practical action was taken. Heavy expenditure was a serious matter when it was all a direct burden on local purses. Despite this lack of progress, the bridge plans had continued to be amended and expanded and the proposed cost had continued to rise. The road width had increased to at least 15.2m, to allow six lanes of traffic (three in each direction) and the estimated cost had risen by 1907 to £718,000.

In the early 1920s, all the factors which had made a new bridge so imperative were redoubled. The High Level Bridge had just been strengthened to carry tram tracks and was increasingly congested; the Swing Bridge was frequently open for river traffic; and road traffic was increasing dramatically in volume. A local civil engineer, T.H. Webster, concealed behind the pseudonym 'Citizen', wrote to the local press pointing out that since the government was intending to advance money to local authorities to fund schemes to tackle unemployment, Newcastle should propose a new high level bridge, rather than frittering away this windfall on small schemes such as widening Benwell Lane.

On the following day Webster's letter found support from Henry Richardson, who felt that 'there is a very strong, though silent, public opinion in Newcastle and Gateshead as to the crying need for a new bridge' and volunteering to act as a coordinator of opinion and eventually to form a pressure group to influence the two councils. A few days later the *Newcastle Chronicle* published plans of Webster's proposals for a new Tyne bridge whose superstructure resembled the King Edward VII Bridge.

Meanwhile, according to the local press of 13 September 1922, an inter-authority group of road engineers known as the North and South Tyneside Joint Town Planning Committee proposed three new Tyne crossings: at Scotswood, near Bill Quay (or Pelaw), and

near the existing High Level Bridge. They also suggested a tunnel between North and South Shields 'later on'. Early in 1923 the Lord Mayor of Newcastle said that it 'was obvious that another bridge was a necessity, and it was only a question of time.' For the rest of 1923, advocates of the new bridge continued to shower councillors and other influential people with plans and speeches, even using the new medium of radio.

The City Council had formed a committee in October 1923 in response to the Joint Town Planning Committee's proposals, and this recommended to the full Council that 'consideration should be given to the construction of a bridge over the Tyne in the vicinity of the High Level Bridge … with a tramway thereon.' The city council's reasons for this change of heart, as expressed by the Lord Mayor, Stephen Easten, were that on Tyneside they had not taken advantage of the government's provisions for subsidising schemes of national importance, the LNER's expression of satisfaction at the increased revenue they were drawing from the High Level Bridge tolls, and that the tramways undertaking (ie the Corporation) was paying the LNER £20,000 a year to use the High Level Bridge. It also appeared that most of the money the government was proposing to spend derived from taxes on motor cars, so the building of a road bridge was an appropriate use.

Having tarried for so long, Newcastle Council moved into top gear, spurred by the fact that it was late in the parliamentary year to start to obtain the necessary Act. In the meantime, Gateshead agreed to a joint scheme and to a division of the costs, the final site was chosen, type and size of bridge agreed and estimates of time and cost calculated. The consent of the LNER, which would have to alter its bridges at either end of the proposed new bridge and which could, after all, expect to lose a large proportion of £20,000 a year, was obtained in principle. There were some protests in Newcastle Council: were they sure the site was the correct one?

Would Pilgrim Street and Northumberland Street become impossibly congested? Were they all rushing headlong towards disaster? All these objections were swept aside by the Lord Mayor and Sir George Lunn, who pointed out that there would be a substantial grant available, and that this was an unrepeatable chance to have a toll-free bridge. After a long debate, the motion to build the bridge was carried on a show of hands 56-0. On 29 April 1924, simultaneous public meetings in Gateshead and Newcastle approved their councils' action.

As the Bill passed through the House of Lords there were several objectors. The local water and gas companies withdrew their objections on being given space on the bridge to carry their mains across. The Tyne Improvement Commission stipulated that there should be a clear height of 25.6m above high water, that a pier in the river was undesirable and that during construction the river traffic should be in no way impeded. (The Tyne Improvement Commission revealed that ultimately, they hoped to have the Swing Bridge removed entirely and the High Level rebuilt with larger spans). The LNER, not surprisingly, was reluctant to give up its toll revenue, and came to an agreement with the city council that the latter should pay a fixed annual fee of £10,000, for which the railway company should cease to charge a toll on tramcars.

With these objections disposed of, the Newcastle upon Tyne and Gateshead Corporations (Bridge) Act received the Royal

The Newcastle abutment, 27 September 1927. The main bearings and bottom sections of the arch are supported on a timber trestle.

By 30 December 1927 the arch was towering above the river.

Assent on 7 August 1924 and work could start in earnest. The estimated cost was £600,000 and the engineers' estimate £550,000, although the cost of land and property would increase the total cost of the bridge to nearer £1m, of which the Ministry of Transport grant was 60 per cent. By December the Joint Bridge Committee had received five tenders: Dorman, Long & Co., £571,225; Cleveland Bridge and Engineering Company, £604,421; Sir William Arrol & Co., £606,454; Sir W.G. Armstrong, Whitworth & Co., £743, 229 and Motherwell Bridge Company, £743, 938. Sir George Lunn pointed out that Armstrong, Whitworth of Elswick's tender was £170,000 above the lowest, and 'local patriotism would not stand the strain of that'.

The bridge was designed by Mott, Hay, and Anderson, based on Sydney Harbour Bridge, designed by Ralph Freeman and in turn derived from the Hell Gate Bridge, New York. The contract for the Sydney bridge had been won by Dorman, Long of Middlesbrough and the Tyne Bridge was also their work. Freeman was consulting engineer.

Construction of the bridge began with the sinking of the concrete supports for the abutments and hinges of the arch, the workmen digging steadily downwards within a caisson under compressed air until bedrock was reached at 24.4m to 27.4m. At the same time as the bridge supports were being built, buildings were demolished for the bridge approaches: in Gateshead, the east side of Bottle Bank and the west side of Church Street were cleared, as well as part of St Mary's churchyard and Bridge Street. This part of Gateshead was the location of many cheap lodging houses; no record seems to have been kept of where the displaced people were moved to.

The road deck was built on each side of the river in 12.2m lengths and hauled by hand winches towards the site of the abutment towers, the deck being added as it moved forward. A light railway on the deck was used to carry materials. As the external walls of the approach would be visible on the Gateshead side, they were faced with second-hand stone blocks taken from the old Newcastle gaol in Carliol Square, then being demolished.

When the upper ends of the arch were finally closed, on 25 February 1928, maroons were detonated and flags unfurled. Total cost of the bridge was about £1,200,000, of which 60 per cent was contributed by the Ministry of Transport. The bridge was painted green with a specially developed paint manufactured by J. Dampney & Company, of Gateshead; the colour was faithfully reproduced in the bridge's repaint of 2000.

The Cornish granite towers above the abutments are of little structural value and were designed as warehouses with five storeys, but the interior floors were never completed, so they were never so used. They also contained passenger and goods lifts to service the Quayside, which was still important to the city's commercial life.

The New Tyne Bridge was officially opened by King George V on the morning of 10 October 1928, although the towers at the Gateshead end were still incomplete. Amid the din of ships' sirens, the royal party crossed into Gateshead for further engagements, while crowds milled around inspecting the new bridge. The King's speech at the opening was filmed by British Movietone News, and the whole construction process had been both filmed and photographed for the contractors.

 ## Who got there first?

It is often believed locally that the Tyne Bridge was the model for the Sydney Harbour Bridge, but this is not so. The contract for the Sydney bridge was awarded in March 1924, that for the Tyne Bridge in December 1924. In Sydney, work on the site began in January 1925, on the Tyne in August. The confusion has probably arisen because the Sydney Harbour Bridge is so much larger than the Tyne Bridge - a 503.1m span as compared with 161.8m, four rail or tram tracks, six motor traffic lanes and two pavements as opposed to four motor traffic lanes and two pavements. In consequence, it was not completed until 1932 - over three years after the Tyne Bridge. The architectural treatment of the Tyne Bridge was by R. Burns Dick although regrettably the massive triumphal arches which he designed for both approaches to the bridge were not built.

Nor were the construction methods used on the Tyne Bridge unique to it. The depth of water in Sydney meant that Freeman had to devise some method of avoiding the use of the conventional staging: his solution, the use of cranes on either side of the arch to advance construction was used also in Newcastle, where the harbourmaster had forbidden the obstruction of the waterway at any time.

After the Tyne Bridge opened, there was an immediate rush of users avoiding the toll on the High Level. After the initial excitement, the traffic crossing, judging from photographs, was light until the late 1950s, but after that morning and evening rush hours began to cause problems. This was exacerbated by the opening of

By 21 February 1928 the arch was nearing completion.

the Central Motorway East and the Gateshead Viaduct in the early 1970s, which created a bottleneck on the bridge. Both Gateshead and Newcastle councils had schemes for a new bridge in this period. The Gateshead idea, which came nearer to fruition, was a part of the A1 Highway, planned in 1966. The northern end of this elevated motorway was designed to cross the railway onto a 'future bridge' across the Tyne to the east of the Tyne Bridge. When completed in 1971, the main road deck of the flyover ended abruptly between the slip roads.

Around the same time, plans were published for a huge motorway network surrounding central Newcastle, part of which was a new 'by-pass bridge' across the Tyne, from which a viaduct would carry the road over the Quayside and City Road, east of Manors Station to link up with the proposed Central Motorway East near Jesmond Station. Although much of the overall plan was eventually carried out, the new bridge was not included.

Linking in with the proposed new bridge east of Tyne Bridge was an innovative plan for a 'Tyne Deck', proposed by the architectural practice of Ryder and Yates in 1969. This was seen as the first step in the creation of a new city of Tyneside, to be formed by amalgamating Newcastle and Gateshead. The river was no longer seen as a boundary between them but a unifying factor, symbolised by the construction of a concrete deck between the two river banks at Quayside level from the Swing Bridge eastwards to the Milk Market. It would incorporate a new bridge running from west of Haggie's Rope Works above South Shore Road to just east of the Wall Knoll Tower. On the deck itself would be built public structures reflecting the unity of the new city. The Tyne

The new Tyne Bridge, its abutments gleaming white, had become the fifth bridge over the Tyne in this aerial view of about 1929.

above the Deck was written off as a commercial river and would be turned into a linear lake for recreation, its waters controlled by sluice gates incorporated in the deck. Although some found these ideas stimulating, the Port of Tyne Authority, the Newcastle and Gateshead Water Company, and other bodies withheld their approval and the Tyne Deck existed as a model only.

The Queen Elizabeth II Metro Bridge

Atunnel under the river, allowing the Metro rapid transit system to serve the area to the south as well as north of the Tyne, was proposed, but that idea was abandoned as too expensive. The Metro Bridge, known for some years only as N106, was built for Tyne and Wear County Council's Passenger Transport Executive, and links Newcastle Central and Gateshead Interchange Metro stations. It stands between the High Level and the King Edward VII Bridges, and like them and the Tyne and Redheugh Bridges, spans the deep Tyne gorge at an elevated level. It was erected between 1976 and 1980 to the design and under the supervision of W.A. Fairhurst and Partners. The contractors were Cementation Construction Ltd. (pierwork), and Cleveland Bridge & Engineering Co. Ltd.(steelwork) who sublet part to Braithwaite of West Bromwich; half the deck units were made locally by Hawthorn Leslie & Co. Ltd.

Described by the revisers of Pevsner as 'rather inelegant (but... presumably cheap)', this bridge (originally intended to be a suspension bridge) is a through-truss steel construction. Individual sections were prefabricated then transported to the site and bolted into position there. Construction was by simultaneous cantilever from each bank until the two sections of the bridge were joined in the centre, on 1 August 1978. The final cost, with approaches and other works, was £6,167,600.

The Queen, accompanied by the Duke of Edinburgh, opened the Metro bridge and the the new section of line from Haymarket station in Newcastle through to Heworth on 6 November 1981. The Metro service over this new section, with its six new stations, was opened to the public on 15 November 1981. The extension from Heworth to South Shields was opened on 23 March 1984. The Metro system is being further extended, from Heworth to Sunderland (due to open in 2002). The enlarged system will undoubtedly add to the volume of Metro traffic and the number of passengers conveyed over the pale green, double-tracked Metro Bridge.

The Queen Elizabeth II Metro Bridge in July 1978.

The Gateshead Millennium Bridge

This stunning new bridge links a reinvigorated Newcastle Quayside with the rebuilt Gateshead Quays, including the Baltic Flour Mills (now converted to the exciting Baltic Centre for Contemporary Art), the Music Centre Gateshead to its west, and the planned housing and recreational developments yet to be erected between them. The Bridge, and the Art and Music Centres, are part of a dynamic programme of development and renewal launched by Gateshead Council which, in partnership with Newcastle Council and with major businesses and organisations on both sides of the Tyne intends to create a 'golden square mile'. The dual-function bridge also creates a mile-long riverside circular promenade using the Swing Bridge, the only other low-level connection between Gateshead and Newcastle.

In 1996 the Millennium Commission announced it was looking for potential landmark projects, to which it was prepared to contribute up to 50 per cent of the cost. Bids had to be submitted by the end of that year, with project completion by 2000. At that time the Gateshead bank was largely derelict, with a crumbling quayside wall, eyesore buildings, the disused Flour Mills, and wasteland behind – but superb views. In August 1996 Gateshead Council made the bold decision to enter the race for Millennium Commission funding and a design competition was announced and launched that month. There were 150 initial expressions of interest, from a variety of companies who came together to create engineering and architectural design teams. Forty-seven teams submitted details of previous work and experience for evaluation. These were eventually whittled down to a short list of six who began to work on their design concepts.

The engineers and architects involved in designing the new bridge were given the brief of creating an attractive structure that promoted the river as a Tyneside asset instead of a barrier separating two communities, while simultaneously maintaining and enhancing existing views. Government approval would be required, the Port of Tyne Authority would have to issue a licence permitting river works, both Gateshead and Newcastle would need to grant planning consent, design and construction contracts would have to

Doug Hall and Lee Smith of Bonneys News Agency, courtesy of Gateshead Council

The Gateshead Millennium Bridge, at Wallsend, is lifted like a toy by the huge Asian Hercules II *crane before the journey up-river.*

be signed, and it was strongly felt that the public should both accept and approve the scheme before any work commenced on site.

A navigation channel 30 metres wide, corresponding to that of the Swing Bridge, would be needed, with 25m headroom clearance when open (equivalent to the Tyne Bridge's deck) and 4.7m clearance when closed (equivalent to the Swing Bridge). Newcastle Corporation stipulated that no permanent bridge support should be built on its Quayside. The curved gradient was to be gentle so that both pedestrians (including those with pushchairs) and cyclists could manage the bridge without difficulty; motor vehicles would be forbidden. The bridge was to take no more than four minutes to open.

The six designs, of varying ingenuity, grace and practicality, were considered by the competition panel – and also by local and national interest groups and independent assessors. One design emerged as a clear favourite with all groups, and the competition winner was announced in February 1997. Professor Tony Ridley, past President of the Institution of Civil Engineers and chairman of the panel judges, described the winning scheme as 'a contemporary design which complements the existing Tyne bridges in a way which is both refreshing and new. Its main arch echoes that of the Tyne Bridge, but it is not a pastiche, it is entirely modern and a fitting tribute to the peak of engineering excellence we are reaching'.

Until the final go-ahead was received from Government there was clearly a limit on what could be done. The Millennium Commission confirmed its funding in April 1998. The Port of Tyne Authority granted its river works licence the following July, insisting on strong fender posts being placed in the river to mark the channel of maximum clearance and withstand the impact of a 4000-tonne ship travelling at four knots.

While Government approval was awaited, the main contractor,

Harbour and General Works Ltd. of Gateshead, was employed in rebuilding the decrepit quay wall. Finally, the requisite Transport and Works Order was received in May 1999 (nine months later than the intended start date – meaning that work could not be completed before the end of 2000, as originally required by the Millennium Commission). Work on the bridge proper began as soon as this Government authority came through.

There were problems encountered in the river, when piling was built on either side; a four-week delay occurred when the Ministry of Agriculture, Fisheries and Food ruled that soil from the riverbed was industrially contaminated. Eventually, foundations and end supports were placed in the river. To facilitate construction two cofferdams were built with two metres of mass concrete in the base to prevent water ingress through the bottom. Altogether, some 19,000 tonnes of reinforced concrete were used in the end supports and the 30m deep foundation piles. The arch and deck were fabricated at Watson Steel in Bolton and the opening mechanism manufactured at Sheffield. From Spring 2000, assembly of the frame (containing enough steel to make 64 double-decker buses) took place in a Wallsend shipyard, with electrical and mechanical connections added on the actual site at Gateshead.

In October 2000 the Dutch floating crane *Asian Hercules II* arrived in the Tyne. One of the world's largest cranes, the 10,650-tonne vessel has an extended jib twice the height of the Tyne Bridge. Three days guaranteed ideal weather were required before the journey up-river from Wallsend to Gateshead could be undertaken. Poor conditions delayed the move, but at dawn on 20 November 2000 the bridge was finally lifted, and rapidly taken up-river – despite its span and tight clearance on the narrower sections of the river. When the crane reached Gateshead and manoeuvred the new bridge into position, the crane operator exhibited enormous skills in managing to lower the bridge to within just one millimetre of its required position! Not only that, but the bridge then had to stay suspended and steady as the tide fell until all 40 bolts were connected to their anchorages. This operation attracted enormous interest locally, and was watched on television by an estimated 100 million people worldwide.

The 850-tonne bridge has been described as simultaneously both robust and delicate. Its design draws attention to the imposing buildings and quaysides on either side of the river, the other bridges and the surrounding riverscape. The bridge span is 126m long. The structure comprises a pair of steel arches, one forming the deck and the other supporting it, the two being linked by thin suspension cables. The designers, civil engineers Gifford & Partners, and Wilkinson Eyre Architects, have used the need to raise the bridge (to allow shipping through at minimal cost – at less than £4 a time) to create a world-first opening mechanism, for it operates like the visor on a helmet, rotating on pivots at each side of the Tyne to form a gateway arch. The main arch rises 50m above river level, almost as high as the top of the Baltic building.

Each of the two concrete piers conceals energy-efficient machinery: electric motors power two hydraulic rams (with a further one in reserve) and the pivots that open and close the bridge. The glass-fronted control cabin is on the Gateshead bank and the bridge staff has CCTV as an additional aid. The bridge is further enhanced at night by a sophisticated lighting system, not only to

The Gateshead Millennium Bridge approaches its final position beside the Baltic Centre for Contemporary Art, the crane towering above the riverside buildings.

illuminate the pathways but also to spotlight the unique design features. Separate sections of the bridge can be illuminated in different colours that can be changed from one hue to another. It is even claimed that, when the new Music Centre building is functioning, it will be possible to change the lighting on the Millennium Bridge in time with the music!

The bridge first tilted on 28 June 2001 (with George Gill, Leader of Gateshead Council, pressing the button) for the passage of a small flotilla of ships and boats (two boats containing pupils representing Gateshead's primary schools). The whole structure rotated through an angle of 40 degrees, creating a gateway clearance of 25m to allow the vessels through. A *Guardian* leader

The Gateshead Millennium Bridge at full tilt, 28 June 2001.

million, with just under half of this (£9.2 million) being contributed by the Millennium Commission. The revolutionary design featured as a first-class stamp issued by the Royal Mail in June 2000 as one of a series to mark the Millennium.

The bridge also features, and is testing, a new type of 'intelligent' paint, developed by the University of Newcastle, which measures the strength of bridge components.

In 2001, *Surveyor* magazine voted John Johnson, Gateshead Council's Director of Design and Construction, its 'Engineer of the Year', for his outstanding work on the Millennium Bridge, from the original concept to the fine result we can all see today. It is the first pivoting bridge

next day saluted recent developments on Tyneside: 'The world's first tilting bridge [has] opened to shipping, not in some exotic transatlantic location but at the heart of a British region long famous for innovation: the North-East. The bridge links Newcastle and Gateshead, two towns which have for so long glowered at each other with unease and suspicion across the Tyne but are now … together growing as bright and thriving as at any time in their history'. By early July over two million 'Cyber Geordies' and others around the world had logged on to Gateshead Council's website to view the bridge's passage upstream, its testing and first opening.

The Gateshead Millennium Bridge was opened to the public on 17 September 2001. The total cost of the project was about £22

of its kind in the world, although a bridge to a similar design is now being built in the United States. The bridge is already a tourist attraction. James Dyson, the famous engineer and inventor of the Dyson vacuum cleaner, has commented: 'I think bridges, when they are properly designed, epitomise perfect structure … When that purity is put into play, as it is in the Gateshead Millennium Bridge, the results are extraordinary … I like the fact that it does not have a straight arch and the shape is oblique. It is a beautiful structure; I love the way you can see exactly how it holds itself up'. Jerry Michell, of the Millennium Commission, describes the bridge as 'a shining example of innovative architecture and design'.

Bridges that were never built

The bridge proposals of 1990-1992

In 1990 a consultants' report suggested three possible crossings between Gateshead and Newcastle: a second Tyne Tunnel alongside the existing one; a new bridge at St Anthony's; or a new low level single carriageway bridge at East Quayside near Spillers' mill. It was claimed that public transport deregulation was partly responsible for the traffic problems: the Tyne Bridge was exceeding its theoretical capacity of 68,000 vehicles a day by over 10,000 and gridlock was predicted for the year 2000. Each local authority picked the one most likely to favour it; for example, North and South Tyneside opted to support the second tunnel, while Newcastle backed one of the two bridge options and Gateshead was neutral. There was also opposition in Newcastle to a bridge debouching into the built-up east end of the city, causing potential environmental problems.

By October 1992, there was an additional Walker to Bill Quay proposal. Central government searched for a private sector partner to help fund any of the crossings as the cost was likely to be upwards of £100 million depending on the option chosen. But it was the requirement of the Port of Tyne Authority for adequate clearances above water level which finally ruled out any of the fixed bridge proposals and the second Tyne Tunnel, although the most expensive proposal, was preferred.

Proposed bridges at St Anthony's, 1845-1992

About 2.5 miles east of Newcastle on the north bank of the Tyne is St Anthony's. In the early 19th century it was a small industrial settlement: opposite it across the river was Bill Quay, a similar village. Between them the Tyne was narrow (particularly so before the Tyne Improvement Commission began to dredge away Bill Point) and its banks relatively low, so this site has always attracted those who wished to bridge the Tyne, while avoiding the expensive land values of the urban areas.

An engraving, published on 11 January 1845, of the proposed railway from Darlington to Berwick showed the line north and south of the Tyne with a gap at Bill Point. Three years later Robert Brandling stated that the plans for a Bill Point Bridge had actually been prepared, and were only abandoned 'in deference to public opinion'. This was not the first scheme for a crossing at Bill Point. Thomas Elliot Harrison, then engineer to the Stanhope and Tyne and the Durham Junction railways, had promoted the idea in September 1836 as part of a scheme to link up railways operating in County Durham.

The financial advantages of bridging in the centre of towns outweighed the disadvantages for the railway companies, and it was not until 1893 that St Anthony's was again considered as a Tyne crossing point. Finally, in 1918 a new railway crossing was being planned there to carry a rail line from Heaton to Washington. In July 1920 Durham County Council agreed to join with Newcastle in pressing for facilities for pedestrian and vehicular traffic to be added to the railway bridge. Various connections with other lines were planned both north and south of the Tyne, and land was bought from Newcastle Corporation and from Lord Northbourne, but the LNER, as successors to the NER, had no enthusiasm for the work and the plans were allowed to lapse. In early 1925 the railway company stated that 'they have not abandoned the proposal … although there is probably very little likelihood of this link being proceeded with in the near future.'

At about the same time, St Anthony's was being considered as the location for a new road bridge to ease congestion in Newcastle and Gateshead. In a report by Mott, Hay, and Anderson and others in 1925, a new steel bridge was suggested from St Anthony's to Pelaw. The size of its main span, at 152.4m, was wide enough to

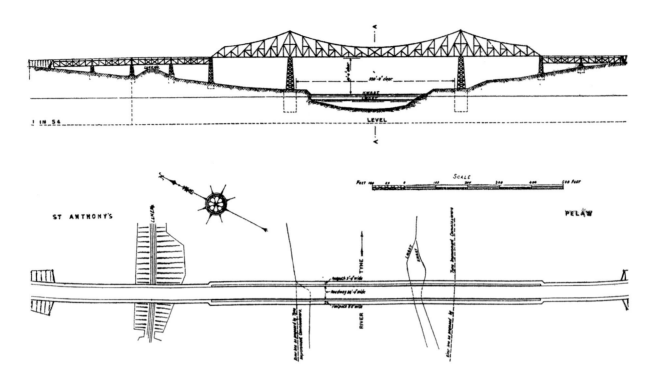

Mott, Hay and Anderson's design for a bridge at St Anthony's, 1925.

allow for the Tyne Improvement Commission's intention to widen the river at this point. At each side was a span of 76.2m, and 38.1m approach spans completed the 533.6m long structure. The deck was wide enough for a 11.6m wide roadway with two 2.7m wide footpaths. The roadway was designed to carry a double line tramway, while water and gas mains would also be accommodated. The steel towers were designed to cope with any mine workings near the bridge and were sufficiently deep to allow the river to be dredged to 9.1m below low water. The approach to the bridge from the north was down Pottery Bank, curving slightly to the east on to the bridge. It gained the south bank just west of Wood, Skinner's ship-

yard. The viaduct crossed Shields Road just east of King Street and crossed the railway and the Ouston wagonway. Then the road divided into two, with one route linking up with Lingey Lane, while the other curved back west to join Sunderland Road where the wagonway crossed it. The total cost was estimated at £928,000. Twenty years later this bridge was still being put forward as a possible scheme in Newcastle's 1945 Plan. A bridge at St Anthony's was last proposed in 1992.

Crossings Below Newcastle (Mid-Tyne)

The Newcastle Quayside-Hillgate, Gateshead Ferry probably existed for many years, used in conjunction with or instead of Tyne bridge. It is shown on a plan as extant in 1831.

 ### The Mid-Tyne Ferries

The Ouseburn Ferry (c.1850-1948),

The Mushroom Ferry (c.1850-1900),

St Peter's Ferry (c.1920-1940), Dent's Hole (roughly St Peter's Basin)-Friars Goose Ferry (c.1831-c.1900),

Felling Shore Ferry (1858-1890)

Heworth Shore Ferry (1858-1900).

The St Anthony's Ferry (1831-1945) was a sculler, later motor-boat ferry (from about 1916). The sculler-boat ferry was deemed unsafe in 1913.

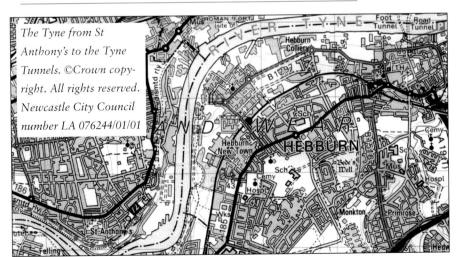

The Tyne from St Anthony's to the Tyne Tunnels. ©Crown copyright. All rights reserved. Newcastle City Council number LA 076244/01/01

There were several small sculler-boat ferries crossing the river downstream from central Newcastle and Gateshead to St Anthony's Point and beyond. Most of these ferries started up as industry grew and developed on both banks. There must have been some bitterness and competition amongst the ferrymen on the river, for 16 'aged seamen of Tyne' appealed in 1870 to have all sculler boats registered and owned only by aged seamen. 'At present young fellows not understanding boats ply scullers, also imposing on seafaring people requiring their services, besides endangering the lives of some.'

Wincomblee Ferry

In 1795 Newcastle Corporation let land at Wincomblee Quay to Edward Redhead, waterman, on which he built a cottage. In 1816 he sought a renewal of the lease, but the Corporation delayed approval until it had enquired into the right of Cuthbert Ellison's lessee to land ferryboat passengers on Corporation land at Wincomblee without paying Newcastle dues. Cuthbert Ellison's lessee was Edward's brother, Anthony Redhead, of Hebburn Quay, who ran the ferry in partnership with Edward. The ferry '… had been held by the petitioner's ancestors for 200 years or more' and Edward was not aware the right of landing and receiving passengers at [High] Walker had ever been questioned. Newcastle agreed to the renewal of Edward's lease in 1822, by which time he was dead and had been succeeded by his son, also Edward. The ferry route is shown on an 1831 plan.

When William Dobson built his shipyard in 1883,

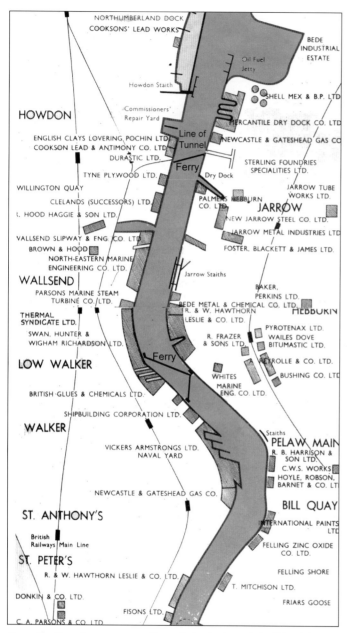

From the Tyne Improvement Commission's plan of the River Tyne, c.1949.

the Corporation Ballast Assessor's office, several cottages and the ferryboat landing were removed to make room for the new yard. This sculler boat ferry appears to have continued to operate from a new site between Dobson's and the Walker Naval Yard until about the Second World War. A mid-19th century plan shows a 'Bill Point Ferry', which may be the same. It was also called 'the Early Ferry'.

Low Walker-Tyne View Ferry (1831-1945).

This sculler boat ferry crossed from the western end of the Neptune shipyard directly across to a point opposite a house called Tyne View.

Wallsend/Walker-Hebburn Ferry

In 1939 the shipbuilding and engineering company, R. & W. Hawthorn Leslie & Co. Ltd, intimated that it would discontinue its ferry services between Walker, Wallsend and Hebburn, established 85 years before. If the figure is correct it indicates that Andrew Leslie started ferry services in 1854, to enable his workmen to reach the Hebburn shipyard he opened the previous year. However it would seem that the firm ran a ferry only between Wallsend and Hebburn from this early date, possibly taking over an existing sculler-boat ferry, whose route is shown on an 1851 plan. In 1903 Hawthorn Leslies bought two second-hand steamers, renamed the *Hebburn* and the *Wallsend*, for this run.

Prior to this, in 1885-1886, just before Andrew Leslie amalgamated with R. & W. Hawthorn & Co., Hebburn and Walker Local Boards (predecessors of local councils) jointly sought to run a horse and cart ferry between the two places, a proposal vigorously resisted by Newcastle and the Tyne Improvement Commission. Although there was a Parliamentary enquiry, the idea foundered. In 1903, Hawthorn Leslie's wished to establish an additional service for its workmen, from Hebburn to Walker. It did not, however, achieve this until 1910. Two smaller boats, the *Fairy Queen* and the *Walker*, were later acquired for the company's two routes.

Early in 1938, Hawthorn Leslie's announced that because of increasing public use of its ferry between Wallsend and Felling, 'constructed' for its workmen, it felt that this should be taken over and run by a local authority. At a meeting of council representatives, the firm's concern was merely 'noted'.

By 1939 the four existing ferryboats were old, and new ones were needed. Hawthorn Leslie reiterated that its ferry services had become a public utility, and should not be left to

The Ferry, Wallsend

The ferry Hebburn *at Wallsend pier, c.1920.*

one firm, itself, to provide. The decision to withdraw the service caused consternation, for it was essential for workers to reach shipyards and other industrial concerns on both banks. Vickers-Armstrong pointed out that new Government orders would soon increase employment. But local firms refused to co-operate and run the ferries together, while local councils did not relish the role either. Hawthorn Leslie's eventually deferred the closure date (originally 30 June 1939) by three months, by which time the country was at war.

From late 1939 the ferry service was operated by a new company, Mid-Tyne Ferries Ltd. of Hebburn, a consortium

supported by the three major shipbuilding and engineering firms, Swan Hunter & Wigham Richardson, Hawthorn Leslie & Co., and Vickers-Armstrong's Walker Naval Yard, together with the switchgear manufacturers and electrical engineers, A. Reyrolle & Co. of Hebburn. Almost immediately, Mid-Tyne Ferries ordered two new boats, *Mid-Tyne No. 1* and *Mid-Tyne No. 2*, delivered in 1940, to replace the *Fairy Queen* and *Walker* (the latter vessel was sold in 1941 and became the relief boat between Howdon and Jarrow). The company had a third boat, *Mid-Tyne No. 3*, built by Hawthorn Leslie in 1949 to replace the ancient *Wallsend*. This venerable steamer was built in 1890 and ran on the Clyde for its

Mid-Tyne No. 2 Ferry on a pleasure trip between Tynemouth and South Shields, c.1950. From Crossley Chronicles, *a magazine produced by Crossley Brothers Ltd. of Manchester.*

exceeded 7,000 per day. There were occasional alarming moments, when the shipyard men, late for work, tried to jump aboard as the ferry was pulling away from the landing stage, and when they scrambled to be the first off the boat in the evening. The three new diesel boats were later given the more imaginative names of *Tyne Queen, Tyne Princess*, and *Tyne Duchess*. From 1945 the Mid-Tyne boats were also used during the summer months for public and private pleasure trips to the Tyne piers and up-river to Ryton Willows. Mid-Tyne Ferries became a subsidiary of the Swan Hunter Group formed in 1968. But the ferries' days were numbered as shipbuilding declined, particularly after the closure of the Walker Naval Yard in 1985. With the *Tyne Queen* making the final crossing, the service ceased on 25 July 1986, by which time only about 200 men were using it each day. The boats have since been used for leisure purposes.

first 14 years before entering into service on the Tyne. Her sister ship, the *Hebburn*, was sunk in collision with a tug in 1940.

The ferries carried about a million and a half passengers annually in their heyday, and during the war years the total sometimes

The Willington Quay/Howdon-Jarrow Ford and Ferries

Unconfirmed evidence exists of a Roman ford at Willington Quay. This is not entirely impossible, for even the lower reaches of the Tyne once obstructed navigation with numerous narrows, sandbanks and shallows. There was a ferry between Jarrow and the opposite bank at the beginning of the 19th century and perhaps before. In 1806 James Jamson and Joseph Jobling admitted infringing Newcastle rights by illegally conveying passengers across the river between Jarrow and Willington Quay, and undertook not to repeat the offence 'nor in any Manner to infringe upon the Right of the said Ferry'. A ferry is said to have operated from the east side of Willington Gut to High Jarrow and there is evidence of this ferry on an 1831 plan. Richardson, in his *History of Wallsend*, states there used to be a sculler boat ferry between Howdon Crane and East Jarrow, and that after Charles Palmer opened his shipyard at Jarrow in 1852 the firm organised a steam ferry between Howdon and Jarrow maintained by two small steamers, the *Punch* and the *Judy*.

However, it seems more likely that the first Jarrow steam passenger ferry was the *Tom Tit*, built by Palmers in 1854, and so underpowered that in a gale it had to beat upstream almost to Hebburn before turning for Willington. The vessel had only a brief life, its 10hp engine subsequently being used in a blacksmith's shop. The 38-ton *Punch* was built for this route by Palmer's in 1861 and sold two years later to the Tyne General Ferry Company, which operated the 'Direct' service between Howdon and Jarrow for the next 45 years. *Punch* may have continued in service on this run until sold to a Penzance man in 1883.

In 1847 the Shields Direct Ferry Company intended to establish a 'Horse and Cart' steamer service between Willington Quay and Jarrow. One source says this started the following year, but it probably began in the 1850s, using *Tyne*. The Tyne Improvement Commission continued to operate the Horse and Cart ferry for some years with this boat. However, when Jarrow borough was incorporated in 1875, it soon considered running a Horse and Cart ferry to the opposite bank. In 1882 it received Local Government Board permission to start this service, which began on 25 April 1883 on delivery of its first steamer; the *G.H. Dexter* (named after the Mayor of Jarrow). The tug *Coquet* was hired to supplement the service until a second purpose-built vessel, the *C.M. Palmer*, was delivered on 13 November 1884. The Jarrow ferry, nearly run down one Saturday afternoon by Charles Parsons' *Turbinia*, travelling at high speed, was one of these boats. In 1899, Jarrow Corporation prevailed on the Tyne General Ferry Company to buy its Horse and Cart ferry service and run it in conjunction with the company's existing ferry.

When the General Ferry Company went into liquidation in 1909, the Howdon-Jarrow ferry was still profitable and this part of its operation was sold. The purchaser was Robert Frazer & Sons of Newcastle, who operated the Horse, Cart and Passenger ferry as a single undertaking for some years. From 1917, however, the company experienced difficulty in making the service pay adequately, and two years later signalled its intention to withdraw. Jarrow Corporation repurchased and ran the ferry again from 10 August 1919.

Jarrow soon commissioned a new, more versatile steamer to replace the *G.H. Dexter* (the *C.M. Palmer* had sunk in 1916). The new ferryboat, the *A.B. Gowan* (named after the manager of Palmer's, whose Amble yard built the vessel), made its trial trip on 9 July 1921. She accommodated 5 lorries or 7 smaller vehicles, and 300 pedestrians (565 without vehicles). The ferry was run on a toll basis until freed by the Ministry of Transport on 1 July 1937; this made a considerable difference (the *A.B. Gowan* conveying 1,412 vehicles between 25 April and 1 May 1937, and 11,365 vehicles

CORPORATION OF JARROW
Jarrow and Howdon Ferries

Revised Tolls and Charges

(Approved by the Ministry of Transport
under date 25th May, 1920)

CATEGORY	DESCRIPTION	FARE
PERSONS.	Passengers	0 1½
	Workmen's Weekly Passes (for 12 journeys only)	0 9
	Workmen's Dinner Passes	0 4½
	Extra Driver or Passenger (all vehicles)	0 1½
GOODS.	Goods under 1cwt	0 1½
	do 1 cwt. or over (per cwt.)	1½
ANIMALS.	Dog	0 1½
	Ox, Cow, or Neat Cattle, and driver	0 9
	Calf, Hog, Pig, Sheep or Lamb	0 1½
	Horse, Mule, or Ass (not Drawing) and Driver	0 6
VEHICLES.	Perambulator, Barrow or Chair, and 1 Person	0 3
	Cycle or Motor Cycle and 1 Person	0 3
	Motor Trailer or Side Car (extra)	0 3
	(2 wheels) Cart and 1 driver	0 7½
	(2 wheels) Trap and 1 driver	0 7½
	(4 wheels) Wagon or Brake, 1 driver and 1 horse 1	1½
	(4 wheels) Wagon or Brake, 1 driver and 2 horses	1 6
	(4 wheels) Wagon or Brake, 2 drivers and 3 horses	2 0
	Heavy Furniture Wagon, 1 driver and 1 horses	1 6
	Heavy Furniture Wagon, 2 drivers and 2 horses	1 9
	(4 wheels) Carriage or Wagonette, 1 driver and 1 horse	1 6
	(4 wheels) Carriage, 1 driver and 2 horses	1 1½
	Motor Car, (two seater) and 1 driver (passengers extra)	0 9
	Motor Car, (four seater) and 1 driver (passengers extra)	1 0
	Motor Wagon, (up to 2 tons) and 1 driver	1 6
	Steam or Heavy Motor Van (up to 5 tons) and 1 driver	2 6

between 15-21 August that year – including some travelling from North to South Shields). By May 1940 the average daily cyclist and pedestrian traffic was 1,230 and 6,400 respectively.

By 1938 the boat's condition had deteriorated so much that vehicles over three tons were prohibited, and Hawthorn Leslie's elderly reserve vessel (the *Walker*, carrying only 160 passengers) was hired (then purchased, in 1941) whenever the *A.B. Gowan* needed an overhaul. The costs of maintaining the ferry had become excessive, despite the Government grant. In 1938 Jarrow Council, hard hit by unemployment, indicated that it had to make economies, and would discontinue the service from the end of the year. The Minister of Transport visited Jarrow and the ferry on 14 November 1938, offering to increase the Government grant to 60 per cent to keep the service going, and upgrade the boat and landing stages; Durham and Northumberland County Councils undertook to find 90 per cent of the shortfall, and Wallsend also agreed to contribute. Jarrow then continued as the ferry authority.

When the Tyne Pedestrian and Cyclist Tunnels opened in 1951, Jarrow Council, having decided to sell the *Walker*, attempted to restrict use of the *A.B. Gowan* to vehicles only but the Tyne Improvement Commission disagreed. In December 1952 Jarrow negotiated to transfer the ferry service to Durham and Northumberland County Councils to operate jointly. The following year the radar-less *A.B. Gowan* was caught in a

The Jarrow vehicular ferry, the A.B. Gowan, *leaving Howdon for Jarrow, 1967*

dense fog in mid-stream for six hours, drifted down-river almost to South Shields, fetching up under the stern of the anchored freighter *Westwood*. The 20 passengers and crew were provided with refreshments aboard the larger vessel until the thick fog cleared slightly, enabling the *A.B. Gowan* to complete its journey to Howdon about 1.30am! The Tyne Tunnel opened on 19 October 1967; the *A.B. Gowan* ceased service that day, made her final crossing on 4 November 1967, and was then scrapped.

The Tyne Tunnels

From before 1930 several road bridge and tunnel schemes had been proposed east of Newcastle, mostly to link North and South Shields. By the mid-thirties the Ministry of Transport was more enthusiastic about a western by-pass and a new Scotswood bridge. The Tyne Improvement Commission opposed the building of a bridge to the east of the city, but was not against a tunnel crossing provided its physical and economic interests were safeguarded.

In 1937, a joint committee of local authorities agreed that a tunnel was the only practicable solution, and wrote to the Minister stressing its national significance. At a further meeting (of Newcastle City, Northumberland and Durham County and Jarrow Borough Councils' representatives), held on 25 January 1938, a new crossing east of Newcastle preferably between Howdon and Jarrow, was thought urgent and necessary. At the minister's behest, on 20 May 1938, another meeting was held, representing all local authorities on the navigable Tyne. The result, a resounding victory for parochialism, was perhaps predictable: Tynemouth and South Shields considered a tunnel could only be between their two

boroughs; Gateshead, Wallsend and Jarrow Boroughs and Hebburn UDC thought a tunnel should be located mid-Tyne; Felling UDC believed a bridge to be better than a tunnel and should run from Felling; Newcastle and the authorities west of the city held no strong views or stressed the need for a new Scotswood Bridge! On 19 November 1938 the Minister visited North and South Shields, saw the ferries and examined the possibility of a tunnel linking the two towns. Despite the Second World War, a decision in favour of a tunnel crossing between Howdon and Jarrow was made in 1943. In 1946 Parliament authorised the building of Tyne Road, Passenger & Cyclist Tunnels; the Ministry gave the go-ahead for work to begin on the two smaller tunnels the following year.

The Tyne Pedestrian and Cyclist Tunnels

The cyclist tunnel was to be west of the pedestrian tunnel, while the larger road tunnel was left until an unspecified future date. On Wednesday, 4 June 1947, the Minister of Transport, Alfred Barnes, cut the first sod. Mott, Hay, and Anderson undertook the design work, with Charles Brand & Son Ltd. as the principal contractor, and Waygood-Otis providing escalators and lifts. The consulting

Tyne Tunnel Joint Committee

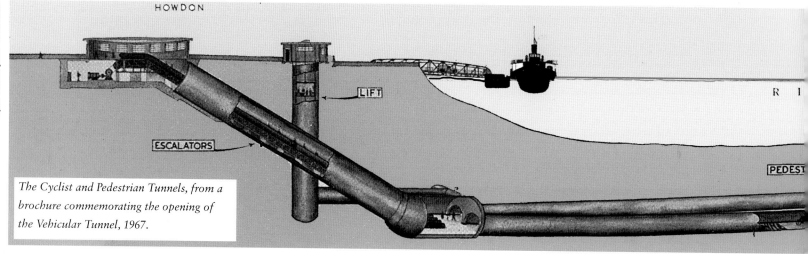

HOWDON

LIFT

ESCALATORS

R I

PEDEST

The Cyclist and Pedestrian Tunnels, from a brochure commemorating the opening of the Vehicular Tunnel, 1967.

engineers' representative, Dr (later Sir) David Anderson, supervised the tunnelling and construction work on behalf of the sponsors, the Tyne Tunnel Joint Committee (of Durham and Northumberland County Councils).

Work took place initially from Jarrow but then from both sides, boring through a complex geological mixture of silt, coarse sand, shingle, sandstone and shale. Progress was unexpectedly slow due to the terrain, taking 597 days instead of the 215 forecast in the contract, and air pressures had to be increased. The Ministry of Transport lent two compressors formerly used at the Dartford Tunnel. The machines were in constant use, day and night, and it is not surprising that they frequently broke down. Two additional compressors were later brought on site. Initially, the two tunnels were pilot bores, later enlarged.

In June 1949 workers discovered fossil remains below the riverbed. They were identified by experts as an elk antler, a deer vertebra and part of a deer horn. Mott, Hay, and Anderson was asked to arrange suitable preservation, with a view to subsequent display; the remains were later offered to the local Natural History Society for exhibition at the Hancock Museum, Newcastle.

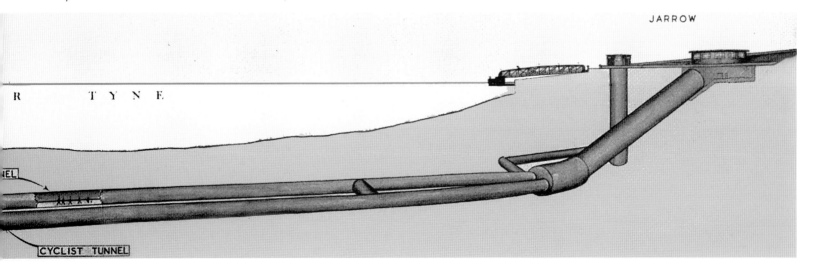

The junction between the Pedestrian pilot tunnel from the Howdon side and the section already driven from Jarrow, 19 May 1949.

On Tuesday, 7 March 1950, the Joint Committee formally celebrated the completion of tunnelling, at a ceremony performed by the Lord Lieutenant of Durham. Ornamental commemorative plaques, including the arms of the two counties, were fitted to the dividing panel between the heads of each pair of escalators. The Committee had already decided to mark the then Durham and Northumberland county boundaries at the mid-point under the river.

The Joint Committee invited a member of the royal family to open the Pedestrian and Cycle Tunnels, but the official reply stated that, as the tunnels were part of a larger scheme, complete only when the road tunnel was built, it would be inappropriate for royalty to be present! Undaunted, the Committee invited the Prime Minister, Clement Attlee, to perform the ceremony when he visited the Durham Miners' Gala in July 1951; unfortunately, his previous commitments prevented this. Shortly afterwards, the Foreign Secretary (a former Minister of Transport), Herbert Morrison, also declined, for a similar reason. On 24 July 1951, Alfred Barnes, who was still Minister of Transport and who had inaugurated the work four years before, declared the tunnels open. The Committee, the Minister and other guests, then marked the occasion with a celebration luncheon at the Royal Station Hotel, Newcastle.

The original estimate for the two tunnels had been £453,150, with a further £164,000 for escalators and lifts, and £16,000 allowed for alterations and additions. With savings achieved elsewhere, the net increase for tunnelling, including wage awards and price increases for materials, was £100,000 and for the escalators and lifts £30,000. The tunnelling and engineering problems encountered, including extra running costs on the air compressors, amounted to another £70,000 – a total of £200,000 over the original contract price.

Once the tunnels were open, everything ran satisfactorily apart from early incidents, mainly due to public inexperience in using escalators. The number of people using the two tunnels gradually decreased from a peak of 25-30,000 per hour on the opening day to an average of 12-14,000 (many of them shipyard workers) each weekday, increasing considerably at weekends. These numbers represented roughly double the traffic previously using the Howdon-Jarrow Ferry. The tunnels quickly recorded their one-millionth user. By early 1952 the average number of users was down to around 7-8000 per day, a figure expected to stay fairly constant. The cost of operating the two tunnels in the financial year 1952-1953 was about £17,000.

A few years later at least one local author thought the whole scheme had been too small-scale: 'the post-war foot tunnel at Howdon amounts to little more than a toy, especially when you look at the steep escalators and the tiny echoing passage, then remember that this is the age of the car and the articulated lorry. So the new bridges and the new tunnel can't come too quickly'.

By 1996, about 7,000 people a week were using the two tunnels. The historic importance and architectural merit of the Tyne Pedestrian and Cyclist Tunnels ensured that they were given Grade II-listed building status in May 2000, and the Cyclist Tunnel is now part of the national cycle network.

The Tyne Road Tunnel

Durham and Northumberland County Councils' Tyne Tunnel Joint Committee was keen to start on the larger Road Tunnel while the Cyclist and Pedestrian Tunnels were under construction. As early as September 1949 the Chairman met the Minister, who was unable to say when money would become available. Protracted delay followed for nine years, while schemes elsewhere were often upgraded to the detriment of the Tyne road tunnel, despite the best efforts of the Joint Committee, local Members of Parliament,

Tyne & Wear Archives

Working on the Tyne Road Tunnel, concreting segments, 12 November 1963.

From the brochure commemorating the opening of the Vehicular Tunnel, 1967, showing the tunnelling shield.

industrialists, civic leaders and others. The need was repeatedly elaborated: the existing, congested, permanent river crossings were concentrated between Newcastle and Gateshead, which for local industrial traffic meant a diversion rather than direct cross-river access; the increase in cross-river traffic exceeded the national average; Pedestrian and Cyclist tunnels were operating, but the Howdon-Jarrow ferry and Shields vehicular ferries had to continue with steamers so old they required frequent overhaul – and the cost of new vessels was excessive. Furthermore, major planning schemes and road development in the area were dependent on the road

tunnel. Land for approach roads had already been acquired; construction plans and contract documents had been prepared by Mott, Hay, and Anderson in 1952, for boring a pilot tunnel, and avoiding sinking caissons.

The Ministry intended Dartford Tunnel shields should also be used for the Tyne and other major tunnel projects but there were long delays before they would be available. Meanwhile, costs rose inexorably, and over time this became another reason for delay. Eventually, matters had dragged on so long that the original legislation had to be extended; the new Act received the royal assent on 5 July 1956.

Despite this, the Ministry of Transport now threw in a red herring, probably on cost grounds: a bridge instead of a tunnel! Local industry reacted strongly and swiftly – if the local economy was to expand the crossing must be built, and soon. The bridge proposal sent everyone scurrying back to their drawing boards – County Surveyors, consulting engineers, the Tyne Improvement Commission and others. In the end it was defeated because of the combined opposition of the Tyne Improvement Commission and the Admiralty. In addition, the engineering problems and cost of a high-level Howdon-Jarrow bridge were daunting. The Tyne Improvement Commission knew a bridge would limit access to the shipyards (including Walker Naval Yard, with a berth capable of building a ship the size of the *Queen Mary*); inhibit the height of vessels on the river, the largest afloat needing mast clearance of

The first wall panels are fitted at the south end of the Tyne Road Tunnel, 23 December 1966.

61m; the bridge piers could endanger navigation, and railways on either bank would complicate the construction of approach roads. The Tyne Improvement Commission stressed that a low-level open-ing or lifting bridge was unacceptable; an alternative, high-level, bridge needed such minimum steep gradients (1 in 17) on the approaches that traffic would have difficulty reaching the 610m road-deck! Felling UDC wrote to the Ministry asking for a bridge between Pelaw and St Anthony's, while other mid-Tyne local authorities continued to press for a Howdon-Jarrow tunnel.

Another problem was the Government's new attitude to tolls. The High Level and Redheugh bridges were made toll-free before the war, with the aid of grants from the Ministry, which also subsidised the Howdon-Jarrow ferry on condition it was free. Since the war Newburn bridge had also been free. But now there was a fundamental policy change: in future tolls would finance the construction, maintenance, operation and debt repayment on all major schemes, with limited Ministry help. The Minister's dictum made the position clear: 'No tolls, no bridge, no tunnel!' The area needed a tunnel; so the Committee reluctantly accepted toll charges.

On 12 March 1958 the Minister finally authorised the Joint Committee to start work on the Tyne Tunnel the next financial year. Since Mott, Hay, and Anderson's original plans there had been some changes: the tunnel carriageway was increased from 6.7m to 7.3m, and the under-river section was lowered to rest entirely on bedrock, with a corresponding gradient increase from 1 in 22 to 1 in 20, and some re-alignment of both tunnel and approach roads. These revisions would reduce the preliminary work from 30 months to 12, although the tunnel would be about 183m longer. There would be no overall increase in price, as the shorter length constructed in compressed air, with other economies, would more than offset the cost of the extended length. The tunnel would initially loop north from the toll collection facility at the Howdon entrance before swinging round on a route south towards Jarrow.

By the summer of 1959 the Joint Committee had approved the tunnel's line, entrances, varied approaches and other revised features. Because of the altered design, further enabling powers had to be authorised by Parliament. When the measures were debated, several motoring and haulage associations objected to the tolls

i Road tunnel facts and figures

The tunnelling shield weighed around 250 tons, had 15 working positions and was propelled by 48 rams, driving an initial pilot tunnel of 3.7m in compressed air conditions, before enlargement to its final dimensions, which were formed with cast-iron segments. The Howdon and Jarrow sections met in February 1965, and by the end of 1966 the tunnel was virtually complete, 1,677.5m long, with an internal diameter of 9.7m. When finished, the two contra-flow carriageways, each 3.7m wide, accessed the tunnel down gradients of 1 in 20. The 183m section under the river bed ran on the level, with the 'crown' or roof of the tunnel 5m clear of the roadway 27.4m beneath the river. On the south side, it was necessary to demolish some housing, and divert the river Don and some sewers through new culverts and pipe work.

included in the new legislation. Nevertheless, the Bill passed, and royal assent was given on 29 July 1960. As with the Pedestrian and Cyclists' Tunnels, invitations to tender were sent out to specialist firms, and by March 1961 the Ministry had approved the contract documents. Work on the Tyne Tunnel commenced on 9 October 1961, with the Minister, Ernest Marples, cutting the first turf. Edmund Nuttall, Sons & Co. Ltd. were the principal contractors. The prior building of the two smaller tunnels provided useful information for this larger project. Work started on the Howdon section, and on the Jarrow section six months later.

The total cost was about £12.5 million, including approach roads and diversionary works. With debt charges, the final figure was well over £22 million; £9 million of this was secured through a long-term loan repaid from toll income; £6.75 million came from central funds, and £2.25 million was raised by the two County Councils; the remaining £4 million qualified for a 75 per cent Government grant, leaving the County Councils to find the other £1 million or so.

The Queen opened the Tyne Tunnel on Thursday, 19 October 1967, and the following day it was in public use. Within a fortnight it had taken more than 50 per cent of Shields vehicular ferry traffic. Six months later there were claims the tunnel was already obsolete – at peak times slow-moving traffic queued up to half a mile on either side. The manager strenuously denied this, insisting the Tunnel was fully capable of carrying 25,000 vehicles a day, and had an average throughput then of 6,500 per day. Back in 1964, traffic density at the outset had been expected to be about 7,000 vehicles daily, rising to a maximum of 20,000 by 1984, with revenue reaching £680,000 annually by 1994. Within two years of opening there were reports of motorists speeding in the Tunnel and in one case, a car driven through at 90 mph, bouncing off the wall four times! Like other major Tyne crossings, the Tyne tunnel has made a significant contribution to the locality's industrial efficiency.

The projected Second Road Tunnel

The need for another road tunnel was foreseen even before the Tyne Tunnel opened; 34 years later, it carries an excessive 35,000 vehicles a day, often creating delays. With all major Tyne crossings now running at full capacity, additional fixed and opening bridge schemes were soon rejected, for height, length, environmental and cost reasons. But firm plans now exist for a second tunnel east of the present one, to carry A19 southbound traffic (the existing tunnel carrying northbound vehicles).

On 31 May 2001, Tyne and Wear Passenger Transport Authority decided to promote this adjacent tunnel, engaging in widespread consultation. With an alternative four-lane proposal no longer viable, an application for a Transport and Works Act Order to construct a two-lane tunnel is to be made, to be followed by a Public Enquiry. If the project is authorised by the Secretary of State for Transport, Local Government and the Regions a consortium will be appointed in 2003, including the PTA's consulting engineers, Ove Arup and Partners (a firm with strong local connections, whose founder was born in Newcastle). The consortium will fund, design, build, maintain and operate the new tunnel, and the existing ones, for perhaps 30 years until costs are recouped. Work is expected to begin in 2004, with completion in 2007 at an estimated cost of £100 million. Tolls will help finance construction.

The new tunnel's middle section will be an immersed tube inserted into the riverbed, a technique increasingly used for safety, speed and cost advantages. Tubular sections will be prefabricated in a dry dock, floated into position, and then lowered into a prepared trench, which will later be covered to prevent possible damage from shipping. The underground access roads at either end will be built using a 'cut and cover' system. Because the new tunnel will not be as deep as the existing vehicle tunnel, the road will not need to spiral down. The second tunnel, if built, should relieve congestion, enabling the Tyne, Swing, High Level and Redheugh Bridges to carry local rather than through traffic.

Crossings between North and South Shields

The story of the crossings between North and South Shields makes best sense if told more or less chronologically.

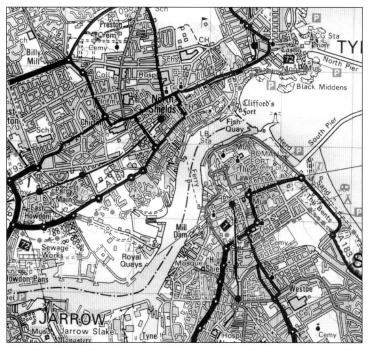

The Tyne from Howdon to the river mouth. ©Crown copyright. All rights reserved. Newcastle City Council number LA 076244/01/01

North-South Shields Ferries before 1800

A ferry between North and South Shields was running by 1377, when Shields men were forbidden to bring in fish on the ferry-boat. In 1588 ferryboat operators were forbidden to land beggars; the ferry stage (the Old Ferry Landing) was then in the Coble Landing area of eastern South Shields, connecting with the Sunderland road. North Shields ferry landing was west of Cliffords Fort, and later at Clive Street. Most ferryboats were for passenger traffic, but in 1588 the 'horse boat' was ordered to be moored with greater consideration to public need, to carry horses, cattle and goods across the river; in 1670 the ferry operators were fined for not keeping the horse boat afloat.

In 1715, Lord Scarborough, commanding the royal troops, confiscated the Shields ferryboats for three days to prevent them falling into the hands of Jacobite rebels. For many centuries the Dean & Chapter of Durham claimed customary rights over the ferries, with powers to lease, and guarded their privileges jealously. In 1729 their lessee suffered grievously when a rival ferry service started; the unlawful competitor was closed down, the Dean & Chapter received £20 in damages – and then refused to renew their tenant's lease! A little later the ferries were apparently leased to Newcastle Corporation whose monopoly was successfully challenged by South Shields' first known shipbuilder, Robert Wallis, who established a fleet of sculler-boats running to and from North Shields.

The Ralph Dodd tunnel proposal, 1797

The first known proposal for a tunnel under the Tyne was in 1797, when the engineer Ralph Dodd suggested linking North and South Shields by this means. At the time the country was at war, and Dodd was at pains to emphasise the military advantages of a tunnel, which would facilitate progress up and down the coast. There would be no need to brave river crossings by boat that could be hazardous when conditions were rough, or by a bridge when it was windy. Furthermore, there would no longer be any need in extreme situations to make the journey all the way inland up to Newcastle to use the Tyne Bridge and then back again down the opposite bank. The dimensions of Dodd's tunnel were to be 366m long on a gentle gradient from Clifford's Fort on the North Shields side to the opposite bank, and with a diameter of 4.3m, sufficient to take loaded wagons. The tunnel would be 'vaulted' with stone and the roadway paved, with lamps and pumps as necessary. It was intended to be a toll-tunnel, and Dodd calculated that it would cost around £7,000 to build.

North-South Shields suspension bridge, 1824-1826

When invasion rumours were rife during Napoleonic times, around 1810, an experimental temporary bridge between North and South Shields was improvised with keel boats, normally employed in carrying coal. The result 'exceeded the most sanguine expectations'. About this time, another successful experiment involved hauling a large, single-deck boat, capable of conveying 300 troops and military equipment, from Clifford's Fort across the river with ropes. There had been no other suggestions for alternative means of crossing the river since Ralph Dodd's propos-

al but the strongest argument was that 18 miles of travel over uncertain roads would be reduced to 366m. In 1821 the population of North Shields and Tynemouth was 9,454 and South Shields 16,500. Communication between the two towns was 'of a primitive kind. Flat-bottomed ferry boats and sculler boats were used for the carriage of passengers and goods and also for horses. The discomfort experienced was very great, and at times the risk of a safe passage was very considerable'. In January 1760 an overloaded boat capsized and ten of its 12 passengers and crew were drowned.

Late in 1824 Captain (later Sir) Samuel Brown proposed a large suspension bridge between North and South Shields. At the time the Menai Bridge, designed by Thomas Telford but using Brown's chain link, was under construction, opening in 1826. Brown's proposed Shields bridge was to run from the west side of (now) Mile End Road, South Shields, across Cook's Quay, to link up with Camden Street in North Shields. There was to be a 22.2m by 12.2m pier on each bank, towering a massive 66.5m above the Tyne, with a main span length of 243.8m and a height above high water at its centre of 35.1m. Each approach had a smaller pier inland of the main abutment to anchor the suspension chains. Captain Brown estimated the cost of the bridge at £93,000 and forecast an annual revenue from tolls at £6,643.

At a public meeting in North Shields on 23 February 1825, it

An engraving of Captain Samuel Brown's proposed suspension bridge from South to North Shields, published with the prospectus in 1825.

was agreed to form an undertaking to build the bridge, a prospectus was published and a committee established. A second opinion was sought from William Chapman, the Newcastle civil engineer, who approved Brown's plans and became, in effect, his local representative. In September 1825, the committee advertised for tenders for the erection of the massive piers of an estimated 600,000 cubic feet of masonry, which had been designed by Chapman and embellished by the Newcastle architect John Green. Within the piers, Green incorporated 'four rooms of excellent accommodation'.

An anonymous letter writer called 'Investigator' made damaging claims in the *Tyne Mercury* beginning on 27 September. 'Investigator' attacked every aspect of the bridge scheme, concluding that since the people of North and South Shields were identical in their habits and occupations, there was no need to build a bridge to link them! The directors asked Thomas Telford to reassure the public. He confirmed that the proposed bridge was a practical proposition.

By November 1825, 83 people had subscribed for 225 £100 shares and soon half the required capital was promised. Despite this promising start, by 10 February 1826 the secretary to the committee announced that they could not apply for an Act of Parliament in the current year, and the idea would have to be postponed. This was, in effect, the end of the bridge. Some thought the southern end too distant from the centre of South Shields, around the Market Place and King Street. Others said that it was due to 'the embarrassed state of the money market'.

Had the bridge been built, it could have had the effect of concentrating much more trade near the river mouth to the detriment of Newcastle. Newcastle, as conservators of the Tyne, had the authority to object to the bridge, but did not. They presumably had no fear that the bridge would ever be built.

The railway age brought further proposals for a link between North and South Shields, though as neither town was on a main route, they were not pursued with any degree of urgency. In 1853, Joseph Locke, a pupil of George Stephenson, proposed an extension to the Blyth and Tyne Railway through South Shields to Sunderland, crossing the river on a high level bridge at 'the lower end of Shields Harbour'. This idea surfaced again in 1864, on this occasion with a high level bridge running from Camden Street to the top of Mile End Road (Brown's route of 1825), with a passenger station in East King Street, South Shields. Although land was purchased in Camden Street, the scheme was dropped.

The Market Place, Direct and Whitehill Point Ferries

When the bridge scheme of 1824-1826 came to nothing, other entrepreneurs quickly stepped in. A private company was formed in 1827 to adapt steamboats as ferries. There was concern in South Shields that scullermen would lose their livelihoods if the project went ahead and that it would limit the choice of crossing points for passengers. But the Shields Ferry Act was passed on 1 June 1829, establishing the North and South Shields Ferry Company, to convey foot passengers for one penny and carriages, horses, cattle, and goods & merchandise at twopence per 50.8 kilos between the two towns. No other ferry exceeding four tons burthen was permitted to operate this crossing. The Dean and Chapter claimed their ferry rights, established centuries before, would be infringed – but accepted one fifteenth of the annual profits in lieu. The company also agreed to pay the Duke of Northumberland 6s 8d per year for landing rights on the north bank.

The Ferry Company was formally constituted in October 1829, with £9,950 capital. Regular services began in July 1830, running between the Market Place/New Quay, North Shields and Ferry Street/Market Place, South Shields (near enough the route still used today). The company's first two steamboats were the *Baron*

A local rhyme described the changeover to the steam ferries

'For threepence to Shields aw remember,
In a wherry the folk used to gan . . .
But now we've got sixpenny steamers,
A stylish conveyance, I'm sure . . .
In sculler boats not very lang syne,
The Shields folk crossed ower the Tyne,
But now that we have got a big steamer,
And cuts quite a wonderful shine'.

A ferry steamer leaving North Shields landing stage c.1900.

Rewcastle, bought in Scotland, quickly found useless, and sold, and the *Durham*, 'a veritable curiosity of naval architecture'. This ferry was built by Oliver of South Shields, with twin hulls joined by an iron stanchion, the gangways raised and lowered awkwardly by winch, and the vessel propelled by a single paddle-wheel in the centre; she carried up to four carts as well as her passenger complement, and took about 20 minutes to cross. The Sunderland-built *Northumberland* replaced the *Baron Rewcastle*; the new boat had a single hull and a marked lack of stability – taking in water whenever when she listed! Both the *Durham* and the *Northumberland* drew about 1.8m of water, and not infrequently ran aground.

Initially, the company was unable to pay a dividend, but by 1835 its trade and profits attracted a 'New Steam Ferry Company', intended to link with the Newcastle and North Shields Railway on the north bank and the Brandling Junction Railway on the south side, both lines then nearing completion. The proposed ferry would run summer and winter, constantly, and at stated times during the night (while the existing ferry did not). However, the scheme fell through. Three years later a 'Tyne Steam Ferry Company' was promoted, with the same objectives, to carry passengers, goods and cattle. Again, the company prospectus failed to attract support.

In February 1847, however, The Tyne Direct Ferry Company was provisionally registered to operate a passenger service between

North and South Shields, using steam vessels of less than four tons burthen, at the existing penny fare. The proprietors first met at the Northumberland Arms, North Shields, on 2 March 1847. The company quickly acquired two small steamers, one, the *Percy*, running a five-minute service from 6am to 10pm from the New Quay, North Shields, to Kinton's Quay (later Comical Corner, near Mile End Road), South Shields. In its first six days the new service is said to have carried 13,296 people. The fare was soon reduced to a halfpenny, and for many years the Direct Ferry was known as 'The Ha'penny Dodger', so called for its efforts to weave in and out of traffic on the river.

The older ferry company sought an injunction to stop the newcomer, who thereupon substituted rowing boats and promoted a Parliamentary Bill to establish a direct steam ferry, with £9,300 in capital and borrowing powers up to £3,100. The new company wished: 'to establish and maintain steam and other boats for… foot-passengers across the Tyne at [North and] South Shields … horses, carts, and passengers between Willington Quay and Jarrow, and … a [passenger] ferry between Whitehill Point, North Shields, and Penny Pie Stairs, South Shields'. The resulting Act contained the unusual proviso that the older company might buy its competitor within 12 months, with authority to raise £8,200 in new capital to achieve this. Purchase and takeover followed, with some directors of the Direct Ferry Company joining the new board, which held its first meeting on the date of amalgamation, 22 June 1849. Although the new company had two good boats and three poor ones, one of the immediate results of the merger was a night service on the Market Place Ferry run.

As early as 1838 and again in 1851, a crossing between Whitehill Point and West Holborn was projected. It actually started on 14 August 1856 when the ferry company founded the service between Penny Pie Stairs (south of Middle Docks and west of Laygate Street, at the Holborn end of South Shields), and Whitehill Point, with the steamboat *Favourite*, for one penny. The Whitehill Point Ferry was largely used by workmen employed by the Tyne Improvement Commission; it barely ran in profit and must have been a drain on the other two ferry services.

In 1861 another in a series of Tyne Improvement Acts passed through Parliament; section 63 empowered the Tyne Improvement Commission to purchase rights in any ferry, establish and maintain any ferry, and charge tolls. This clause was inserted largely on the initiative of Tyne Improvement Commission representatives from Shields, who perceived an opportunity to acquire what was regarded locally as an inefficient service. Following this, and despite the lukewarm feelings of other Commissioners – and the ferry company's natural hostility – a section was included in the Tyne General Ferry Act the next year, authorising the Tyne Improvement Commission to purchase the Shields Ferry Company at an independently-arbitrated price. The Commissioners took over the three ferries for £39,000 on 1 May 1863, and established the North and South Shields Ferry Company. At this point the vessels in use were for horse and cart traffic: the *Durham* and the *Northumberland* (Market Place ferry), and the *Tyne* (Jarrow ferry); with the *Percy* on the 'Direct' (passengers only); and the *Favourite* on the Whitehill Point (passenger) run. The Tyne Improvement Commission immediately spent about £20,000 on new boats and improved ferry landings. In 1865 another Act enabled the Tyne Improvement Commission to buy and extinguish all the ancient ferry rights previously exercised by the Dean & Chapter of Durham.

After the defeat of the transporter bridge scheme in 1901, (see page 109) the Tyne Improvement Commission, which had been heavily criticised, agreed to promote a Bill in the next Parliamentary session enabling it to upgrade its ferry services. Legislation was enacted in 1902, and included provision for

A vehicular ferry (Market Place), possibly the Tynemouth, *at North Shields landing stage c.1900.*

improvements to the ferries, the landing stages, and the service generally. Two new, larger, floating stages were provided at North Shields. The west section divided to cater for Market Place passenger and vehicular traffic respectively, and the east section provided for the Direct Ferry, and the General Ferry Company's steamers. A new larger floating stage was built at South Shields for the Market Place Ferry, again divided into two sections for passenger and vehicular traffic. The Market Place Ferry was be carried on by new, fast, specially-constructed steamers, with separate steamers for vehicular

and passenger traffic.

Despite the promises of 1901, it was strongly felt that the service deteriorated after 1906, with only passenger traffic benefiting (a 10-minute service as against 30 for the vehicular ferry). In 1912 the Tyne Improvement Commission took a long, hard look at its finances and increased fares on the vehicular ferry by an excessive 50 per cent. There was strong resistance, but from 1863 to 1910 the Tyne Improvement Commission had made little or no allowance for depreciation on its ferryboats and plant. During the period 1891-

North-South Shields ferrymen, c.1935. The emblem on the gansey, right, reads 'Shields Ferries T.I.C.'

1900 income apparently exceeded expenditure by over £3000 per year, and from 1900 to 1910 by about £4000 each year. The real figures, allowing for capital expenditure and depreciation, were very different. Another attempt was made in 1919 to increase fares generally, but was partially withdrawn after protests. In 1925 the Tyne Improvement Commission sought to increase fares at will (instead of a statutory five-year review) or to sell off the ferries to Tynemouth or South Shields Councils, or anyone else.

Economic reasons may not have been the only cause of the decline of the ferries. They were unpopular amongst many Tynemouth/North Shields and South Shields inhabitants; both borough councils castigated the service in 1938 for its inefficiency, saying that it was totally inadequate for important occasions such as major football matches, useless when suspended because of fog and

at night when it no longer ran; it irritated other river traffic when it cut directly across their paths. Furthermore, Newcastle and Gateshead together had a population of half a million and five bridges, whilst North and South Shields had 200,000 and neither a bridge nor a tunnel. Even worse, if a tunnel was eventually built between Howdon and Jarrow, the Shields ferries would still be necessary. It has even been suggested that another reason for decline was a change in licensing laws. For many years, in some areas, only genuine travellers were allowed to buy a drink; to circumvent this legislation, people would board the Shields ferries, purchase a return ticket and show it to the local publican to prove they were a real traveller and so entitled to a drink! Whatever the truth of this, the Shields ferries sometimes carried unusual cargoes, amongst them circus elephants, chained to the bulwarks!

The author James Kirkup, looking back on his childhood, described the two main ferries running from his home-town of South Shields across to North Shields. One, he said, was a small boat called 'the Ha'penny Dodger' (the Direct Ferry) while the other (the Market Place Ferry) was a far grander affair, with gleaming white lifebelts, an upper deck where you could watch the captain at the wheel, and a saloon with upholstered seats. The ferry trips were exciting: through the stiff, noisy turnstile and then running down the jetty and on to the gently-rocking landing stage; watching with bated breath as the great ferry berthed, the crew vigorously hauling on the ropes to pull her in; then the passengers would clamber on board, the siren would blast, the engines throb, the signals ring; then ropes were cast off, and the boat would slowly, very slowly, turn round and head into the river. A late arrival would be marooned on the floating stage, and the South Shields houses and docks would gradually seem to drift away; the ferry would reach mid-river, and a gale would be blowing from the sea. How could anyone possibly sit reading newspapers in the saloon...

Between 1921 and 1928 the Tyne Improvement Commission ferry revenue and expenditure exceeded £300,000, with net profit averaging less than £3000 per year. But in addition the Tyne Improvement Commission was involved in capital expenditure on the ferries in excess of £100,000 per annum from 1926 to 1929.

	1881	1919	1929	1935	1942
Market Place	[P] 1,683,698 (+1831)	c.3,000,000	3,327,524	2,963,809	3,113,141
	[V] n/a	c.175,000	166,549	268, 598	99,986*
Direct	[P] 899,194 (+963)	n/a	782,561	387, 580	369,112
Whitehill Point	[P]143,561 (+10,406)	c.600,000	392,847	225,193	193,093**

P: passengers V: Vehicles. + season tickets shown separately *1941 total. **1940 figures; 162,642 to 30 September 1941, when the Whitehill Point Ferry was suspended due to enemy action.

The bow points towards the landing at North Shields; the ferry arrives alongside; the voyage is over too soon; the passengers disembark.

Ordnance Survey and other plans indicate that the route of the Whitehill Point ferry changed at least eight times over the years between 1860 and 1951, originally running straight across from Penny Pie Stairs to Whitehill Point, by degrees moving on a more north easterly route until by 1927 it ran to the eastern end of the Tyne Commission Quay, inside the approach to the Albert Edward Dock. In 1951, its route is shown from the east side of the Albert Edward to the Market Place landing in South Shields. Following its withdrawal due to damage in an air raid in 1941, the Whitehill Point service was reinstated on 1 April 1951 for an experimental period, using the steam launch *Osmia*. Parliamentary approval was obtained to abandon the service, which ceased altogether on 30 September 1952.

The next year permission was sought to discontinue the Direct Ferry, which made its last sailing on 28 August 1954. The 'Ha'penny Dodger' had ceased after running for 107 years; the *Collingwood* went to a Cornish shipyard, to be converted into a luxury yacht. An application by a South Shields boatbuilder to continue the Direct service, using a motor launch, was refused. The Market Place vehicular ferry had been carrying about 400,000 vehicles a year; when the Tyne Tunnel opened in 1967 this figure fell to just a trickle; a helicopter to carry passengers between the two towns was suggested in place of the boats. In March 1968 the 57-year-old ferryboat *South Shields* was withdrawn and broken up, followed next month by the 43-year old *Tynemouth*, leaving just the 39-year old *Northumbrian* to maintain the service until a new passenger-only diesel ferry was built, at Ryton Marine, Wallsend, for £60,000.

This was the twin-screw diesel vessel *Freda Cunningham*, named after the wife of the chairman of the Tyneside Passenger Transport Executive that had taken over the ferry service from the Port of Tyne Authority (previously Tyne Improvement Commission) on 1 May 1972. The *Freda Cunningham* made her first trip on 6 May 1972; three days later her engines broke down –

Ferryboat Northumbrian *at the Market Place Landing, North Shields c.1960.*

diesel vessel, the *Shieldsman*, was designed to be more resistant to nets, ropes, and other flotsam in the river. *Shieldsman* has no bows or stern, but has identical ends. This avoids the need to turn before setting off again, provides increased stability, and saves fuel, wear and tear; the propellers steer as well as drive the vessel through the water, giving *Shieldsman* far more manoeuvrability. She came into service in September 1976, as the principal ferry, with the *Freda Cunningham* demoted to reserve.

In 1994 another modern diesel ferryboat, the *Pride of the Tyne* was built by Swan Hunter's (the last boat built by the 'old' Swan Hunter yard), to supersede the *Freda Cunningham*, which was then sold. The *Pride of the Tyne* cost £1.5 million, including £300,000 European grant aid. This 200-tonne ferry can carry up to 350 passengers on ferry crossings, and up to 250 on river cruises. By 1994 the ferry service was conveying about 800,000 passengers per year.

the first of many occasions, resulting in modifications and much 'preventative maintenance' (when the ferry failed to operate, a bus service took passengers via the Tyne Tunnel). The *Northumbrian* was withdrawn, converted into a floating restaurant, and for a time moored at Gateshead.

Towards the end of 1974, approval was given for a new ferry-boat; the contract went to Hancock Shipbuilders Ltd. of Pembroke Dock, South Wales and building started early in 1975. This new

Proposed North-South Shields road bridges

After 1826 all subsequent crossing ideas were for road bridges. In 1887 a joint committee of South Shields and Tynemouth councils met to consider a bridge, but made no progress. In 1893 J.R. Lawson, a South Shields councillor, proposed a bridge, but failed to convince the Tyne Improvement Commission that it would not obstruct river traffic. This was the usual fence at which North-South Shields bridge plans fell. In 1901, the Shields Bridge Company was incorporated for the purpose of building a transporter bridge to run from Howard Street, North Shields, to Mile End Road on the south bank. The bridge was of a proven French design and a secondary objective was to link up the tramway systems of the two towns. Initially, the proposal passed scrutiny by a House of Lords Committee on 27 March, despite strenuous opposition from the Tyne Improvement Commission (which said it intended greatly to improve its ferry service), but was rejected by a House of Commons Committee on 3 July 1901.

On 6 May 1901, while the transporter bridge idea was still alive, the local paper printed details of a notion by an anonymous 'local engineer', who proposed a remarkable bridge design for the crossing: this was a stiffened suspension structure with a deck 64m above high water at spring tides, accessed by inclined railways carrying cars large enough to hold horse-drawn vehicles and tramcars. While this notion certainly got around the Tyne Improvement Commission's problems with the clearance for large vessels and also the length of approach viaducts necessary to meet their objections, the scheme seems to have had other problems and no more was heard of it.

The subject was not raised again until the successful scheme for the new Tyne Bridge between Newcastle and Gateshead was begun. The fact that this had been made possible by a 65 per cent grant from the Ministry of Transport caught the attention of those who were interested in a river crossing at Shields and from 1925 a great number of ideas was put forward, both official and from interested individuals. In 1926, Councillor E.F. Jackson proposed a huge cantilever structure, resembling the Forth Railway Bridge, running from Howard Street in North Shields, to the inevitable Mile End Road, South Shields. The design's single central span of 243.8m incorporated a drawbridge at its centre, which when opened gave a clearance of 76.2m above mean sea level, which Jackson hoped would appease the Tyne Improvement Commission. The new bridge would be of more than local importance, as it would link south-east Northumberland with Teesside.

In addition to his advocacy of a bridge, Jackson argued for a tube railway or tunnel and deprecated the Tyne Improvement Commission's ferry service as expensive and slow. The cost of the bridge was estimated as £750,000 to £1 million. These sums were almost small change when compared with the cost of the bridge designed by the borough engineer of South Shields, J. Paton Watson, early in 1929, estimated to cost £2 million. Watson had the usual dig at the ferries: if they were to continue, he

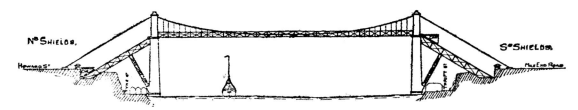

SHIELDS BRIDGE.—AN ALTERNATIVE PLAN.

The anonymous scheme for a Shields Bridge, Shields Gazette and Shipping Telegraph, 6 May 1901.

J. Paton Watson's bridge from the Shields Daily News, *5 January 1929.*

storey car parks, would have been sited at Mitre Street in South Shields, which was in the area to be levelled under slum clearance powers and 'on the North side no property of great value is affected'. The bridge itself was to be another Forth railway bridge type, a single span cantilever 298.7m long and 19.3m wide, with no tram tracks.

Following the publicity for Watson's bridge, several would-be bridge designers rushed into print with their plans. First was J.W. Hodge, a South Shields haulage contractor, who proposed a Forth railway bridge-type cantilever with a main span of 274.3m, the approaches commencing at West Percy Street, North Shields and ending in Mile End Road, South Shields. This bridge was to be 23.8m wide: a model of it was displayed which was still available 40 years later during another period of public agitation for a bridge. Hodge was followed a few days later by Herbert W. Boyce, who suggested what was probably the most radical idea of the period, for a double swinging cantilever bridge from Mile End Road to Howard Street. When swung open, the two halves would leave a gap of 192.9m. This would be a rare occurrence, as the bridge deck was to be 27.4m above high water, adequate for most river traffic. As well as being about one third of the cost of the two rival plans,

reckoned 'they should be taken over by that Department of Government which is responsible for the maintenance of ancient monuments, and run free of charge to users'. The bridge versus tunnel argument was also rehearsed, but the main obstacle to a bridge continued to be the clearance required above river level (this time given as 56.4m, which would require an approach 1,158.8m long on the South Shields bank starting at Ogle Terrace). Watson proposed to overcome this problem by approaching the bridge proper by a huge spiral ramp, 121.9m in diameter and 30.5m high at each end: 'one would scarcely realise having travelled the spirals before reaching the bridge'. These vast ziggurats, not unlike multi-

ANOTHER SCHEME TO PROVIDE BETTER COMMUNICATION BETWEEN BOROUGHS.

MR HERBERT BOYCE'S PROPOSAL.

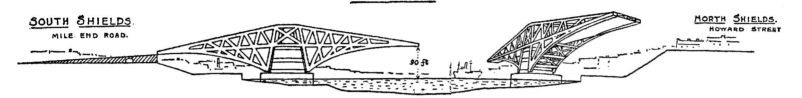

Herbert Boyce's proposed bridge, from the Shields Daily News, *January 28 1929.*

Boyce's bridge would be one third the height, and therefore 'a much less conspicuous target for the enemy's guns from the sea'.

While these schemes of varying merit were being proposed, the local councils, led by South Shields, became involved in a practical way. A conference on 15 February 1929 at South Shields Town Hall decided to ask the Minister of Transport whether he would be prepared to pay part of the costs involved in 'obtaining a report from an Engineer as to the best method of providing a crossing for passenger and vehicular traffic over or under the River Tyne between South Shields and North Shields to link up with the highways, and if practicable the railways on both sides of the River to form an additional trunk route from North to South along the coast, with a design, plans and estimates of the cost of the scheme recommended, and what amount of grant the Minister would be prepared to make towards the cost.'

A deputation visited the Ministry in May 1929 and the Divisional Road Engineer was asked to report. Eventually a grant was approved from the Road Fund to cover the cost of an engineer's report. Terms of reference were drawn up and a fee of 1,500 guineas offered in April 1930. The engineers (Mott, Hay, and Anderson) reported in 1931 that the cost of a bridge would be high

compared with that of a tunnel, which was estimated as £1.24m. The Minister of Transport warned that the government grant would not exceed 60 per cent of this figure, leaving the local authorities, in the midst of an economic depression, to find the remainder of the cost, to which would have to be added the costs of approach roads to the tunnel. The local authorities also faced the intractable opposition of the Tyne Improvement Commission to any bridge which might interfere with the river's trade. Thus in May 1931 all dreams of a bridge link between the 'harbour boroughs' in the foreseeable future died.

Two proposals for bridges between South Shields and Tynemouth survive in the archives, both dated in pencil September 1930. One is for a bridge forming part of a 'North East Arterial Highway', crossing the Tyne at Whitehill Point. It is an almost exact copy of the then recently completed Tyne Bridge. The other is a more conventional bridge with long approaches running from Albion Road in North Shields to the Municipal Buildings in South Shields.

But the idea of a bridge between North and South Shields has refused to die. There was some agitation in 1971, but it was not until the advent of the National Lottery, which appeared to make

Sketch plan of about 1930 for part of a 'North East Arterial Highway' with this bridge, strongly resembling the Tyne Bridge, crossing the river at Whitehill Point (Royal Quays on the map on page 100).

the journey in two minutes. Electric lifts were to be provided at each end of the line, and the railway was intended to provide a 24 hour service. The Parliamentary Bill was passed unopposed on 17 March 1902 and received the Royal Assent. The idea persisted for some years, and in 1906 the North and South Shields Railway Act was re-enacted to extend the construction time to 31 July 1910. The project was revived in 1914, with a new Parliamentary Bill; by this time the envisaged route was a continuation south of Bedford Street, North Shields, under the river, to surface just west of Mile End Road. First World War priorities were probably the main reason for the abandonment of the scheme.

all dreams possible, that the idea was revived. This was a 1996 proposal for a footbridge 152.4m high and half a mile long, linking the piers.

North-South Shields tunnel proposals, 1902-1936.

Some of the advocates of the transporter bridge had another string to their bow in the form of an electric railway running in a 4m diameter tunnel or tube under the Tyne, proposed in 1902. A company with a projected £200,000 capital was formed to construct this railway running from Bedford Street, North Shields under the Tyne and emerging at the junction of Mile End Road and Stanhope Street. The tunnel was to be for passenger traffic only, the electric trains leaving the terminus every six minutes, completing

However, the prospect of a light railway connection between the two boroughs did not disappear for good. In 1922 and for several years afterwards, an ingenious Australian engineer, Elfric Wells Chalmers Kearney (the son of a Newcastle-born minister) promoted a high-speed railway, an idea he had been working on since 1902. Kearney's electric light railway scheme was for a monorail link under the river in a 4.6m diameter tube between North and South Shields. The two-car train was to be for passengers and parcels only, and would be kept in place by retaining wheels on a rail above ('the Kearney system'). Gravity would enable the train to pick up speed quickly, by having steep inclines (1 in 7!) either side, with an estimated journey time of just 50 seconds. A three-minute service in each direction was possible but every five minutes more likely. Cars would have doors on both sides at eight-seat intervals to facilitate access and exit.

Kearney optimistically estimated that about five million people per year (figures based on Shields ferries traffic returns) would use his railway, and this would increase with time. At twopence per trip this would bring in £41,666 in its first full year, while anticipated running costs (power, maintenance, staff, depreciation and rates) would amount to only about £10,000. There was substantial enthusiasm for the project, particularly in South Shields Council, and at one time Kearney was asked to adapt his proposal so that vehicles could also be carried; but this would have doubled the cost (originally estimated at £300,000) so was dropped by 1925. Kearney reckoned tunnelling under the Tyne could be done for about £200 per 91.5cm run, with 'cut and cover' construction on the two land approaches.

As time went on, there were concerns about the safety of the Kearney scheme: that the tunnel might be too shallow on the North Shields side and the vibration of the trains could damage the tube and the riverbed. Moreover, the Tyne Improvement Commission would lose perhaps £16,000 a year on its passenger ferry operation, while the vehicular ferry would have to be maintained. A provisional light railway order was granted, but the final order was refused when this went before a House of Commons Select Committee in 1928. South Shields had continued to give the project warm support but Tynemouth's enthusiasm had evaporated. The Tyne Improvement Commission said it was not opposed to a tunnel, but it wanted an adequate and properly-financed scheme that took account of the ferry situation. Kearney returned to Australia between 1929 and 1933, but then came back to Britain, and in 1934 collaborated with Arthur Whitley Ltd. in a new scheme to construct a tunnel for his high-speed railway with a highway for vehi-

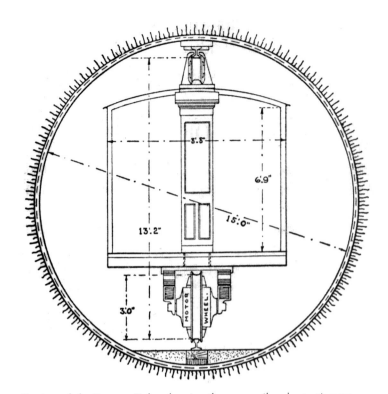

Section of the Kearney Tube, showing the monorail and retention systems, about 1924.

cles. Tynemouth and South Shields both objected to his new North and South Shields Railway Company acquiring control of the vehicular ferry. The Tyne Improvement Commission was in favour.

By 1930 there were plans for a road tunnel under the Tyne, east of Newcastle. The consulting engineers, Mott, Hay, and Anderson, came up with four designs dependent on size and cost, for a tunnel connecting North and South Shields. These were amongst a number of bridge and tunnel proposals current at the time. Shipping and other business interests regarded a tunnel as the only viable prospect. It could have helped entrepreneurs who had wished to

gradient and an internal diameter of 8.4m allowing a maximum vehicle headroom of 4.9m, to start near the New Quay in North Shields and terminate at Waterloo Vale, South Shields. This would cost £1,300,000 to build, plus £100,000 compensation to the Tyne Improvement Commission to abandon its ferries. The annual maintenance cost would be about £7,000.

On 7 February 1936, a deputation from Tynemouth and South Shields boroughs, met the Minister of Transport, Mr Hore-Belisha, who felt the case for a road tunnel was not strong enough. When asked if anything could be done to improve the North-South Shields ferry service, the Minister reiterated that the tunnel should be postponed, although he agreed the ferries might be improved.

North and South Shields, site of the bridges and tunnels that never were, c.1950.

start firms on Tyneside but had been deterred by the poor infrastructure (a 20-mile detour to cross the river, or use the antiquated ferry service) and had set up elsewhere. Some of these were businessmen who had expressed interest in taking over recently-closed shipyards. The preferred tunnel design was Mott, Hay, and Anderson's B1, a 1,281m tunnel, with a single sidewalk, a 1 in 20

The suggested train ferry, 1899

In November 1899 a local newspaper correspondent, John Wilson, suggested a train ferry from Mill Dam, South Shields, across to Albert Edward Dock, thereby connecting the riverside railways that ran along the north and south banks of the Tyne. However, nothing came of the idea.

Up and Down River Services and Crossings

There may have been ferries on the Tyne in Roman times, working from the important fort, Arbeia, at South Shields, handily placed for troops and stores from the continent but not an integral part of Hadrian's Wall. Arbeia was later used as a supply depot to service the Wall, perhaps including the easternmost fort, Segedunum, at Wallsend and probably forts further west. By 300 AD the Arbeia garrison is known to have included sailors, marines and bargemen from the river Tigris, and it may be that they were involved in ferrying supplies by boat to distribution points up-river.

The early steamers

From early modern times barges, wherries, open boats and then 'comfortables' (partially-covered rowing boats) were available to people travelling between different points on the Tyne, as well as for the conveyance of goods, often for some distance. But on 19 May 1814 a great novelty, the *Tyne Packet* steamboat, joined the annual Ascension Day parade of vessels proceeding from Newcastle down the Tyne. The following month, the vessel, whose name was soon changed to *Perseverance*, began a spasmodic ferry service connecting Newcastle and South Shields, the first such passenger and goods service in the country. She was soon joined by the *Swift* and on 25 February 1816 the *Eagle* steam packet, plying each day 'as the tide serves' (best cabin one shilling, fore cabin sixpence). But the returns were poor, and after two years the boats were laid up; from 1818 they were used by Joseph Price as the first tugs. However, by 1831 more than 30 steam vessels were plying for intermittent hire between Newcastle and the mouth of the river.

In 1838 the Newcastle and Shields Steam Packet Company was set up to operate a regular steamer service 'with handsome and powerful steam vessels', to do the journey in an hour, for sixpence, compared to the existing 'dirty and uncomfortable' steamboats that took three to four hours. Its boats also competed with 15 horse-drawn gigs, five omnibuses and three coaches then running between Newcastle and North Shields, taking an hour to an hour and a half and charging one shilling and sixpence or two shillings. The company's vessels, *Tulip* and *Daisy*, began a two-sailings-a-day service from the Tyne Bridge to the New Quay, North Shields, on 15 October 1838, improved to four times a day on 24 November. This was augmented within a month by a third boat, the *Dahlia*, which

'Jemmy Johnson's wherry', presumably a 'comfortable', an illustration from a popular 19th century song.

enabled the company to increase the frequency of service to almost hourly, from 8.45am to 3.45pm. The timetable was improved still further the following February (with each vessel making three return trips daily), and July.

Enthused by the Packet Company's success, the Port of Tyne Steam Navigation Company's 'fast and splendid steamers' *Sun*, *Planet*, *Star*, *Comet* and *Mercury* began a similar service. Competition was evidently keen, for the Steam Packet Company announced that it would run a half-hour service, from 7.30am to 5.30pm, for fourpence, from 7 October 1839. The riposte was swift: the Port of Tyne company immediately announced a reduction in its fares from 12 October 1839 to sixpence 'in the After Cabins and on the Quarter Decks', and fourpence 'in the Fore Cabins and on the Decks'. The Steam Packet Company confirmed its half-hour service, reminding passengers that its vessels (with the *Violet* and the *Rose* now added to its fleet) were all furnished with stoves and suitable accommodation. Perhaps there were too many boats, for two months later the Steam Packet Company issued a handbill stating the *Violet*, *Tulip* and *Rose* ran just twice a day and that goods were carried on very moderate terms. The *Rose* and the *Tulip* were used to convey passengers on a pleasure trip from Newcastle to view the launch of the *Bucephalus* at St Peter's on 2 April 1840.

The Tyne General Ferry Company

In August 1859, following Charles Palmer's ferry service from Jarrow to Mill Dam, South Shields, which began that July, John Rogerson started a regular passenger steamer service with six large boats (the Red Star Line) from Newcastle Quayside to Prior's Haven, Tynemouth, with calling stations in between on both sides of the river. According to location in the boat, the fare was twopence or threepence for the full journey. The Shields Ferry Company opposed the new 'up and down river' service, and sought an injunction to stop the Red Star steamers (and those of a rival concern, the Percy or Crescent Line, set up by J.R. Lawson of South Shields) plying their zigzag route from bank to bank – both lines were also using the Mill Dam landing in South Shields. Because there was insufficient traffic – and therefore profit – for all the ferries, Rogerson (part-owner of the shipbuilding yard at St Peter's) and his fellow directors, applied for an Act of Parliament which was

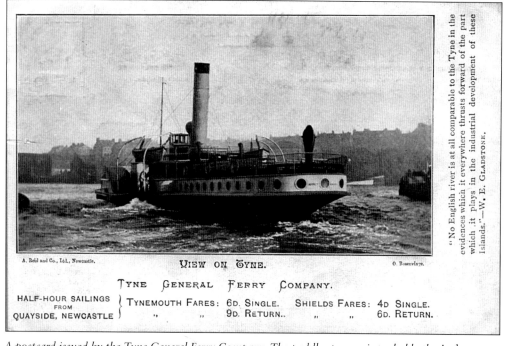

"No English river is at all comparable to the Tyne in the evidences which it everywhere thrusts forward of the part which it plays in the industrial development of these islands."—W. E. GLADSTONE.

A. Reid and Co., Ltd., Newcastle.   O. Rosenvinge.

VIEW ON TYNE.

TYNE GENERAL FERRY COMPANY.

HALF-HOUR SAILINGS FROM QUAYSIDE, NEWCASTLE } TYNEMOUTH FARES: 6D. SINGLE.   SHIELDS FARES: 4D SINGLE.
,,   ,,   9D. RETURN.   ,,   ,,   6D. RETURN.

A postcard issued by the Tyne General Ferry Company. The paddle steamer is probably the Audrey, *about 1900.*

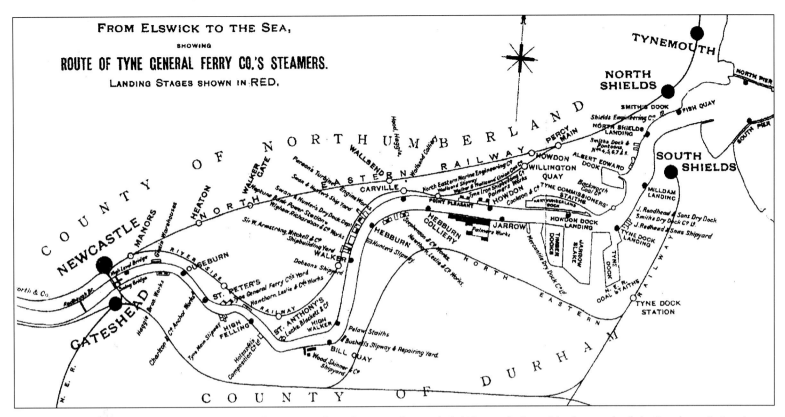

By 1903 the 20 vessels in the company's fleet had calling points along the river. These included Newcastle Quayside, the mouth of the Ouseburn, St Peter's, High Felling, Bill Quay, High and Low Walker, Hebburn, Wallsend, Hebburn Colliery, Howdon, Jarrow, Howdon Dock, Tyne Dock, Mill Dam, North Shields and North Shields Fish Quay (plus the piers, up-river, and coastal excursions during the summer season).

passed in 1862. This incorporated the Tyne General Ferry Company, with a capital of £60,000 and £20,000 borrowing powers, to provide and use steam vessels to convey people, animals and goods along the Tyne within the Tyne Improvement Commission jurisdiction. It also exempted the company from the provisions of the Shields Ferry Act.

The new firm absorbed the Red Star Line, and built some landing stages. (The Tyne Improvement Commission had, under far-reaching powers in its 1861 Act, acquired the right to control ferries, and to erect landing stages.) Business boomed. In 1870 there was an unsuccessful attempt to establish another ferry company to run a service between the incomplete Tyne piers. The Tyne General Ferry Company then operated that route for almost 40 years as an extension to its usual summer schedule, but largely at a loss. Nevertheless, when the company ceased operations, others were keen to take over the route.

By 1872 the Tyne General Ferry Company's regular half-hour service had proved to be cheap, quick, comfortable and reliable (soon superseding some 'direct' or cross-river ferries along the river), and calling at landing stages on both banks from Elswick and Dunston above Newcastle down to North and South Shields.

It must once have been profitable, for in 1872 the company carried around 4 million passengers a year; by 1899 this had increased to almost 7 million, but from that time on the totals gradually dipped each year until in 1907 it was almost back to the 1872 level. From 1865 income rose from around £26,000 per year to £44,000 in 1899, but gradually dropped down to £30,000 in 1907, with expenditure (such as the increasing cost of coal) outpacing revenue and paring profits. Too little allowance was made for depreciation on its boats. In 1907 the company made a profit of just £448, but also had a bank overdraft of over £25,000.

The fall in the company's fortunes was, however, due mainly to growing competition from riverside railways and tramways on both banks. The ferry company had pioneered workers' cheap tickets,

 ### General Ferry Company steamers

General Ferry Company paddle steamers included the *Garibaldi, Robert Chalmers, Stamper, Tynemouth; Mary Jane, Walker* (both 1862); *Louise Crawshay* (1863); *Harry Clasper, Eliza* (both 1864); *Jarrow, John Edwin, Joseph Cowen, Loftus Perkins, Sarah Rogerson* (all 1865); *Charles Atwood* (1881); *Lady Florence* (1882); *Beatrice, John Clayton* (both 1883); *Alice* (1887); *Doris, Isabel* (both 1889); *Wallsend* (1890); *Eleanor* (1891); *Mabel, May* (both 1891); *Phoebe* (1895); *Aileen, Audrey* (both 1897),supplemented in 1903 by the first twin-screw *Mona*.

but once the NER followed suit the ferry company was in deep trouble. After an Extraordinary General Meeting on 2 May 1908, the General Ferry Company announced that it would have to discontinue its by then 17-station up-and-down river service from 31 October that year. There were frantic efforts by local authorities, chambers of commerce, and leaders of industry to persuade the Tyne Improvement Commission to take over the company, or to finance the service from local authority revenues. Workers and employers on both sides of the river would be badly affected.

The Tyne Improvement Commission was unwilling to be further involved in the ferry business, despite its well-equipped yard at Howdon for the upkeep of plant such as ferryboats and landing stages. Disposing of the Ferry Company's yard at St Peter's would reduce costs and rationalise the service with the existing Tyne Improvement Commission ferries. The Tyne Improvement Commission had increased landing stage charges, and there seems little doubt the company was unfairly treated. Even when powerful voices such as Sir Andrew Noble of Armstrong's, and local newspapers such as the *Newcastle Chronicle* and the *Shields Gazette*, wrote that an up-and-down/cross-river service was essential, the Tyne Improvement Commission still refused to enlarge its role. It did offer to remit landing stage rents for three years while several local authorities offered to indemnify the Tyne Improvement Commission against loss if it agreed to continue the service. Despite the Ferry Company (with bank approval) agreeing to delay closure, there was insufficient willingness and resolve in any quarter to maintain or underwrite the service; the last up-and-down ferry ran on Saturday 5 December 1908. Sixteen steamers were laid up and 200 employees were out of work.

In February 1909 the company stated it needed £10,000 capital to restart, with a further £65,000 from local municipalities, repaid at four per cent per year over 20 years; the latter sum would enable the company to purchase six new boats and acquire the assets of the old company, with the local authorities being sole shareholders. The company also approached the largest firms along the river but deemed the replies unsatisfactory. A local authority joint committee reluctantly recognised that the cause was lost. The Tyne General Ferry Company went into liquidation and was finally wound up on 4 May 1909, and Tyneside lost for good what in its heyday had been a wonderful work-day and leisure service.

But that was not quite the end. In 1909, a firm in Berwick provisionally enquired about the service. Early in 1910 a prospectus was issued for a Tyne Ferry Company, to revive the up-and-down river service, using ten motor launches each about 13.1m in length, running at about 9.5 knots and carrying up to 60 passengers between Elswick, Dunston, Newcastle and other stations down to North Shields. The prospectus pointed out that the previous company had used far larger vessels than necessary, which were uneconomic on coal consumption and crew numbers. The new boats would have three-man crews against five for the old company. However, the proposal won insufficient support, partly because the new company sought similar concessions from local authorities.

Interestingly, however, in the spirit of the old Tyne General Ferry Company service, the idea of a river bus operation was suggested in 2001, with boats calling at 18 ferry landings between Blaydon and the river mouth.

On board a Tyne General Ferry Company ferry, about 1900.

Aerial Crossings

The earliest flight over the Tyne seems to have been that of C. and G. Green, in a balloon, on 30 May 1825. The 'daring aeronauts' rose in their 'vast machine' of crimson and white silk from a packed Nun's Field in Newcastle to the accompaniment of 'bands of music'. The balloon headed south towards Chester-le-Street. They flew over the whole of County Durham before landing near the Tontine Inn and Mount Grace Priory, north east of Northallerton, 48 miles away. Half the gate money went to local charity. The Greens made several flights from Newcastle around this time, but this seems to have been the only one over the river.

Soon after the Wright brothers' successful flight in 1903, local aeronautical pioneers and their supporters in the Northumberland and Durham Aero Club discussed (in 1910) whether a 'flying ground' should be based at Blagdon, Boldon or Gosforth Park, for local and visiting pilots. In 1911, the *Daily Mail* organised a round-Britain air race, with a £10,000 prize. One control point on the second leg, from Hendon to Edinburgh, was Gosforth Park. On Monday 24 July, there was a queue half a mile long to enter the park to see the planes fly in from Harrogate, passing over Durham, Chester-le-Street and Newcastle. Unfortunately, of the 17 pilots who left Hendon that day, only four (two Frenchmen, Jules Vedrines and the eventual winner 'Beaumont' – Jean Couneau – followed by two Britons, James Valentine and a Mr Hamel) reached Gosforth Park on the Monday and only one, Samuel Cody, the following day. The second Briton to arrive, Hamel, veered off course, almost colliding with the Penshaw Monument, arrived over the Tyne and Newcastle before realising it, and crash-landed at

MESSRS C. & G. GREEN
ASCENDED
From Newcastle upon Tyne,
Wednesday, 11th May—Monday, 23rd May—Monday, 30th May
And MESSRS G. & W. GREEN
On Thursday, 14th July,
1825.

Burradon. After strut repairs he was able to fly back to Gosforth Park. Cody had crashed at Brandon, Durham, but came on the next day after repairs, crossing the Tyne to the west of the city. At 7am he was seen over South Gosforth at a low altitude, the whirr of his engine being heard long before he arrived. Cody was awarded the Northumberland and Durham Aero Club's prize by its president, Sir Charles Parsons, for the first British-made aircraft to arrive.

Armstrong's opened their first airship works at Selby in 1915. By 1925 it had a factory at Cramlington making airship components, with an airship hangar at the airfield there. There is evidence of Armstrong's airships flying over the Tyne from around 1920.

Amongst the more notable airship events was the sighting of the British airship *R101* over the area in November 1929. Leaving her base at Cardington, Bedfordshire, she set out on her seventh and longest flight to date, flying over England, Scotland and Ireland. Shortly after 4pm on Sunday, 17 November, she 'shook Newcastle out of its Sabbath afternoon somnolence'. Thousands, 'disturbed from their afternoon siesta by the drone of the huge engines', flocked into the streets to watch. There were murmurs of admiration and delight when she was caught in the golden rays of the setting sun, on a course over Heaton towards Tynemouth, about 457.2m up. The *R101* entered Tyneside via Durham and Birtley, passing slowly and very low, down the Team Valley and over Bensham, where it turned over the city and then made towards the coast. The *R101* tragically crashed into a hill in France, with the loss of 48 lives, the following year.

Tyne & Wear Archives

R33 *over the Tyne entrance, about 1920 (this may be a composite photograph).*

In August 1931, the German airship *Graf Zeppelin* completed a cruise over Britain and Ireland, flying over Tyneside on her way south from Scotland: 'Early morning mists partially shrouded the *Graf Zeppelin* when she passed over Newcastle at about 8.45am but crowds of men and women [glimpsed] the majestic airship. With her gondolas brightly illuminated, the huge dirigible presented an imposing appearance as the silver-grey silhouette was seen limned against the heavens. At Ryton, probably on account of the fog, she had been flying very low, little more than 100ft up when she passed over the village … One of the best views was from near the … Central Station'. Apparently taking the Tyne as a guide, she passed over Jarrow and South Shields a few minutes later, before turning south for Sunderland and Middlesbrough. The giant German airship *Hindenburg* crashed in New Jersey in 1937, again with severe loss of life, effectively ending the role of this form of transport.

In 1916, illustrations appeared in German newspapers, and a special commemorative postcard was issued, purporting to be views of an airship raid over Tyneside. One picture showed the airships over the Tyne bridges, while another depicted Elswick works in flames. But the raid never happened – the propaganda was intended as a morale-booster. However, a South Shields resident could recall being picked out of a cot to watch a zeppelin glide over Westoe Village, and drop a bomb near South Shields Market Place.

There were airships in the area on 15 June 1915 (South Shields and Jarrow) and 2 April 1916 (South Shields and Whitley Bay).

During the Second World War at least one major German bombing raid took place on Tyneside shipyards and industrial installations; stray planes often used the Tyne as a navigational aid and on occasion jettisoned bombs in unsuccessful attempts to hit the bridges.

The first internal and international scheduled civil flights in the area, were from Cramlington around 1930, and from Woolsington (now Newcastle International Airport), which opened in 1935. Woolsington was requisitioned by the RAF in 1939, and domestic and overseas flights were resumed in 1947. Many of these flew over the Tyne, as they continue to do in increasing numbers today.

AirFotos

A view from the air: the Tyne and its newest bridge, 20 November 2000.

Details given vary slightly according to the source used. Figures derived from several sources including TWCC Bridges statistics, c.1983.

CROSSING	DATE	TYPE	LENGTH	WIDTH	DESIGNER	CONTRACTOR	COST
BRIDGES							
High Level	1846-49	Rail	229. 2m	12.2m	R Stephenson & T.E. Harrison	Rush & Lawton (masonry)	£491,153
	1846-50	Road	229. 2m	12.2m		Hawks, Crawshay (ironwork)	
Swing	1868-76	Road	142. 5m (Swing 85.7m).	14.48m	John Ure (TIC)	Sir W.G. Armstrong	£288,000
King Edward VII	1902-06	Rail	334. 4m,	15.25m	C.A. Harrison (NER)	Cleveland Bridge Co.	£500,000
Tyne	1925-28	Road	161. 8m	17.08m (+ 2.7m footpaths)	Mott, Hay & Anderson	Dorman Long & Co.	£1,200,000
Redheugh	1980-83	Road	360m	15.8m	Mott, Hay & Anderson	Edmund Nuttall Ltd.	£15,350,000
Metro	1976-81	Rail	360m	10.31m	W.A. Fairhurst & Partners	Cementation Construction & Cleveland Bridge Co.	£6 million
Gateshead Millennium	1998-01	Pedestrian & Cycle	126m	8m	Gifford & Partners, Wilkinson Eyre	Harbour & General	£22 million
Scotswood	1964-1967	Road	178. 5m	20.13m	Mott, Hay & Anderson, with City Engineer	Mitchell Construction & Dorman Long	£1.7 million
Blaydon	1990	Road	332m	14.6m	Bullen & Partners	Edmund Nuttall Ltd.	£17 million
Newburn	1892-1893	Road	126. 4m	8.54m	Sandeman & Moncrieff	Head Wrightson & Co.	n/a
TUNNELS							
Tyne	1947-1951	Pedest. & Cyclist	274.5m	3.05m 3.66m	Mott, Hay & Anderson	Charles Brand & Son	£833,000
Tyne	1961-1967	Road	1.7km	9.53m	Mott, Hay & Anderson	Edmund Nuttall Ltd.	£22 million

NAME	ROUTE	PURCHASED	REPLACED/SOLD
Baron Rewcastle	Market Place	1829	c. 1830
Durham (no. 1) [P]	Market Place	1831	1866/1869
Northumberland (no. 1) [V]	Market Place	1830	1883 1889
Tyne (no. 1)[V]	Jarrow	1844	1869 (converted to floating hospital)
Percy [P]	Direct	1862	1894 (spare),1896 (converted to steam tug)
Favourite [P]	Whitehill Point	1856	1868 (spare), 1876
Durham (no. 2) [V]	Market Place	1866	1897 (converted to floating crane to assist pier work)
Shields [P]	Whitehill Point	1868	1903 (spare), 1905
Tyne (no. 2) [V]	Market Place	1869	1911
Tynemouth (no. 1) [V]	Market Place	1883	1921 (spare),1924
John Usher [P]	(used as spare)	1876 (converted tug) ...	
J.C. Stevenson [P]	(used as spare)	1883 (TIC vessel) ...	
J.R. Proctor [P]	Whitehill Point	1890	1926 1928
Northumberland (no. 2) [V]	Market Place	1896	1926
Collingwood (no. 1) [P]	Direct	1896	1939 (Sea Scouts base, Willington Quay, 1943)
George Armstrong [P]	Direct	1904	1927
Thomas Richardson [P]	Market Place	1906	1930
U.A. Ritson [P]	Market Place	1906	1930
South Shields [V]	Market Place	1911	1968
Tynemouth (no. 2) [V]	Market Place	1925	1968
Durham (no. 3)[P]	Whitehill Point	1926	1941 (bombed during air raid and scrapped)
Northumbrian [V]	Market Place	1930	1972
Collingwood (no. 2) [P]	Direct	1939	1954
Osmia (TIC Launch) [V]	Whitehill Point	1951	1952- service ceased
Freda Cunningham [P]	Market Place	1972	1994
Shieldsman [P]	Market Place	1976-	
Pride of the Tyne [P]	Market Place	1993-	

[P] = Passenger; [V] = Vehicular Ferry

Bibliographical note

Every factual statement in our text is supported by a reference to our source material, but it seemed to us that to give these in full would unnecessarily clutter up the text for most readers, so we have deposited fully annotated copies in Tyne and Wear Archives Service and the Local Studies Section of Newcastle City Library, where those interested can consult them. What follows is a list of the books and articles we found most useful.

Of the general local histories, the most useful for its area, which contains much information on the Shields ferries, is George B. Hodgson, *The Borough of South Shields* (1903, reprinted 1996).
S. Middlebrook, *Newcastle upon Tyne: its Growth and Achievement* (1950; reprinted 1968).
W. Richardson, *History of the Parish of Wallsend* (1923, reprinted 1998).
F.W.D. Manders, *A History of Gateshead* (1973).
Blaydon Local History Society, *A History of Blaydon* (1973).
Richard Welford, *A History of Newcastle and Gateshead* (3 vols., 1884-7) were also of use.
Valuable general surveys are: N. Pevsner, *The Buildings of England: Northumberland* (revised edition, 1992).
R.W. Rennison (ed)., *Civil Engineering Heritage: Northern England*, (2nd. ed., 1996).
I. Ayris & S. Linsley, *Guide to the Industrial Archaeology of Tyne and Wear* (1994).
We also found W.W. Tomlinson, *The North Eastern Railway* (1914, reprinted 1967), Martin Smith, *British Railway Bridges and Viaducts*, (1994) and Ken Hoole, *Rail Centres: Newcastle* (1986) helpful.
On the Tyne Bridges, J. Collingwood Bruce, *The Bridges and Floods of Newcastle upon Tyne* (1887) and R.F. Hindmarsh, *Some of the Tyne Bridges* (1927) are still of interest. Fuller technical details may be found in the following:
High Level Bridge: R.W. Rennison, 'The High Level Bridge, Newcastle: its evolution, design and construction', in *Transactions of the Newcomen Society*, vol. 52 (1980-81).
John Addyman, and Bill Fawcett, *The High Level Bridge and Newcastle Central Station: 150 years across the Tyne*, (1999)
Swing Bridge: Tyne and Wear Industrial Monuments Trust, The Tyne Swing Bridge (1976).
Redheugh Bridges: The director's minutes of the Redheugh Bridge Company, dealing with the first and second bridges, are held by Tyne and Wear Archives. The current bridge is described in J.D. Lord and others, 'The new Redheugh Bridge' in *Proc. Inst. of Civil Engineers*, Part 1 (1984) 76 May, 497-521, and in Tyne and Wear County Council, *The New Redheugh Bridge* (1983).
King Edward VII Bridge: F.W. Davis and C.R.S. Kirkpatrick, 'The King Edward Bridge, Newcastle-on-Tyne', in *Minutes of Proc. Inst. of Civil Engineers*, vol. 174 (1907-08), pp 158-187.
New Tyne Bridge: David Anderson, 'Tyne Bridge, Newcastle', in *Minutes of the Proc. Inst. of Civil Engineers*, 230 (1929-30), pp 167-202.
Stafford M Linsley, *Spanning the Tyne: the Building of the Tyne Bridge 1925-1929*, 2nd. ed. 1998.
T.H. Webster, *The New High Level Bridge and its Origin*. 1928.
H.Y. Richardson, *Proposed New High Level Road-Vehicle and Foot-Passenger Bridge from Pilgrim Street, Newcastle-upon-Tyne to High Street, Gateshead* (1923).
Scotswood Bridge: D.W. Smith, 'New Scotswood Bridge' in *Proc. Inst. of Civil Engineers*, vol. 42 (February 1969), pp217-249.
Queen Elizabeth II (Metro Bridge): P. Layfield and others, 'Tyne and Wear Metro Bridge: bridge N106 over the River Tyne' in *Proc. Inst. of Civil Engineers*, Part 1 (1979) 66 May, pp. 169-189.

Generally, local newspapers, particularly the *Gateshead Observer* and the *Shields Daily News* and the Newcastle dailies contain much information, as do the printed proceedings of Newcastle Council from 1836 and those of the Tyne Improvement Commission from 1874. Further unique records of most of the crossings are to be found in the holdings of Tyne and Wear Archives.

Indexes